CliffsNotes™

The Old Man and the Sea

By Jeanne Salladé Criswell, M.F.A.

IN THIS BOOK

- Learn about the Life and Background of the Author
- Preview an Introduction to the Novella
- Study a graphical Character Map
- Explore themes and literary devices in the Critical Commentaries
- Examine in-depth Character Analyses
- Enhance your understanding of the work with Critical Essays
- Reinforce what you learn with CliffsNotes Review
- Find additional information to further your study in CliffsNotes Resource Center and online at www.cliffsnotes.com

D0029399

Wiley Publishing, Inc.

About the Author

Jeanne Salladé Criswell has written numerous critical essays, stories, poems, newspaper articles, speeches, and other professional communications and has served as a college teacher, writer, editor, communications director, and editorial manager. She owes everything to her parents, George and Nancy, and her beloved husband, Mark, and extends her appreciation to Tammy Castleman, Diane Smith, Greg Tubach, and her patient and dedicated editor, Tracy Barr, for their help with this book.

Publisher's Acknowledgments

Editorial

Project Editor: Tracy Barr

Acquisitions Editor: Greg Tubach

Glossary Editors: The editors and staff at Webster's New World Dictionaries

Editorial Administrator: Michelle Hacker

Composition

Indexer: York Production Services, Inc.

Proofreader: York Production Services, Inc.

Wiley Indianapolis Composition Services

CliffsNotes™ *The Old Man and the Sea*

Published by:
Wiley Publishing, Inc.
111 River Street
Hoboken, NJ 07030
www.wiley.com

Copyright © 2001 Wiley Publishing, Inc., Hoboken, NJ

Library of Congress Control Number: 00-107698

ISBN: 978-0-7645-8660-6

Printed in the United States of America

15 14 13 12 11 10 9 8

1O/RQ/QZ/QS/IN

Published by Wiley Publishing, Inc., Hoboken, NJ

Published simultaneously in Canada

Table of Contents

How to Use This Book

This CliffsNotes study guide on *The Old Man and the Sea* supplements the original literary work, giving you background information about the author, an introduction to the work, a graphical character map, critical commentaries, expanded glossaries, and a comprehensive index, all for you to use as an educational tool that will allow you to better understand *The Old Man and the Sea*. This study guide was written with the assumption that you have read *The Old Man and the Sea*. Reading a literary work doesn't mean that you immediately grasp the major themes and devices used by the author; this study guide will help supplement your reading to be sure you get all you can from *The Old Man and the Sea*. CliffsNotes Review tests your comprehension of the original text and reinforces learning with questions and answers, practice projects, and more. For further information on Ernest Hemingway and *The Old Man and the Sea*, check out the CliffsNotes Resource Center.

CliffsNotes provides the following icons to highlight essential elements of particular interest:

Reveals the underlying themes in the work.

Helps you to more easily relate to or discover the depth of a character.

Uncovers elements such as setting, atmosphere, mystery, passion, violence, irony, symbolism, tragedy, foreshadowing, and satire.

Enables you to appreciate the nuances of words and phrases.

Don't Miss Our Web Site

Discover classic literature as well as modern-day treasures by visiting the Cliffs Notes Web site at www.cliffsnotes.com. You can obtain a quick download of a CliffsNotes title, purchase a title in print form, browse our catalog, or view online samples.

How to Use This Book

CliffsNotes Hemingway's *The Old Man and the Sea* supplements the original work, giving you background information about the author, an introduction to the novel, a graphical character map, critical commentaries, expanded glossaries, and a comprehensive index. CliffsNotes Review tests your comprehension of the original text and reinforces learning with questions and answers, practice projects, and more. For further information on Ernest Hemingway and *The Old Man and the Sea*, check out the CliffsNotes Resource Center.

CliffsNotes provides the following icons to highlight essential elements of particular interest:

Reveals the underlying themes in the work.

Helps you to more easily relate to or discover the depth of a character.

Uncovers elements such as setting, atmosphere, mystery, passion, violence, irony, symbolism, tragedy, foreshadowing, and satire.

Enables you to appreciate the nuances of words and phrases.

Don't Miss Our Web Site

Discover classic literature as well as modern-day treasures by visiting the Cliffs Notes Web site at www.cliffsnotes.com. You can obtain a quick download of a CliffsNotes title, purchase a title in print form, browse our catalog, or view online samples.

You'll also find interactive tools that are fun and informative, links to interesting Web sites, tips, articles, and additional resources to help you, not only for literature, but for test prep, finance, careers, computers, and the Internet too. See you at www.cliffsnotes.com!

LIFE AND BACKGROUND OF THE AUTHOR

The following abbreviated biography of Ernest Hemingway is provided so that you might become more familiar with his life and the historical times that possibly influenced his writing. Read this Life and Background of the Author section and recall it when reading Hemingway's *The Old Man and the Sea*, thinking of any thematic relationship between Hemingway's work and his life.

Early Years

Ernest Miller Hemingway was born the second of six children in Oak Park, Illinois, on July 21, 1899. His mother, Grace, was a religious woman with musical talent, while his father, Clarence Edmonds ("Ed") Hemingway, was an outdoorsman who loved hunting and fishing in the northern Michigan woods. From an early age, Ernest shared his father's interests. He also vacationed with his mother on Nantucket Island and heard tales of his seafaring great-grandfather, Alexander Hancock. Much of what Hemingway learned in the early years about the outdoors and nature's lessons became the basis of many of his stories, such as some of the Nick Adams stories and *The Old Man and the Sea*.

Hemingway attended Oak Park and River Forest high schools, where he wrote for the newspaper and the literary magazine and participated in sports such as boxing, swimming, and football. He didn't attend college but instead began working as a reporter for the *Kansas City Star*. Later, he also wrote for the *Toronto Star* and *Star Weekly*. His early journalistic career profoundly impacted his literary writing style, which was always honed and spare.

Experiences and Literary Achievements

Hemingway was rejected for regular military service in World War I because of a weak left eye, so he drove a Red Cross ambulance in Italy, distributing chocolate to Italian troops. While recuperating from serious wounds in a Red Cross hospital in Milan, Hemingway fell in love with nurse Agnes von Kurowsky, who later rejected him as too young. These World War I experiences eventually became invaluable fodder for his most famous war novel, *A Farewell to Arms*. The experiences contributed to many of his war novels' recurring themes: the cruelty and stupidity of war, the greedy materialism and quest for power that cause war, the platitudes and abstractions that glorify war, and the value of enduring whatever must be endured.

As a foreign correspondent for the *Toronto Star Weekly*, Hemingway moved to Paris. Armed with a letter of introduction from Sherwood Anderson to Gertrude Stein, Hemingway established friendships with a number of famous expatriate writers who helped him develop his craft. Hemingway published *In Our Time*, a collection of short stories, some of them the Nick Adams stories set in Michigan. In 1923, Hemingway made the first of five consecutive yearly trips to Pamplona, Spain, for the bullfights —an experience that eventually served as a basis for *The Sun Also Rises*, which is about the expatriate life in Paris and Pamplona. In the epigraph of that book, Hemingway quotes a line that Gertrude Stein previously recounted: "You are all a lost generation." The phrase "lost generation" quickly became a mantra of the post World War I generation's attitude about the war's effect on their lives and the futility and meaninglessness of life.

In 1928, Hemingway moved to Key West, Florida, and began deep-sea fishing. That same year, his father committed suicide. In 1932, Hemingway went on a two-month fishing expedition to Havana and began marlin fishing, which eventually provided material for *The Old Man and the Sea*. In 1933, he continued fishing off the coast of Cuba, sailed to Paris, and then went on to Africa for a safari in Kenya and Tanganyika. The safari provided a setting for *Green Hills of Africa*.

As a foreign correspondent in Paris, Hemingway began to raise funds for the Loyalist cause in Spain. In 1937, he went to Spain as a war correspondent covering the Spanish Civil War, which gave him material for *For Whom The Bell Tolls*, his best-selling novel about an American volunteer and a band of Spanish Loyalist guerillas. Hemingway's goals in the book included a clear depiction of the indifference of the world's democracies to encroaching fascism and the desperate need to fight against it.

In 1939, Hemingway moved to *Finca Vigia* (Lookout Farm), a house near Havana, Cuba. When World War II began, he volunteered to serve as a spotter for the U.S. Navy, outfitting his own fishing boat, the *Pilar*, to hunt for German submarines off the Cuban coast. In 1944, he became a war correspondent for *Collier's* and covered the war, including the liberation of Paris, with the U.S. Fourth Infantry Division. "Papa" Hemingway, as he was dubbed, purportedly liberated the Ritz hotel in Paris, particularly the bar, just prior to the arrival of Allied troops.

After the war, Hemingway married his fourth wife, Mary Welsh, a *Time* magazine correspondent. Drawing on his World War II experiences, he published *Across the River and Into the Trees*, about a May-December romance. A subtle consideration of war in modern times, this book was less realistic and more symbolic than his previous work and was roundly attacked by critics. However, his 1952 publication of *The Old Man and the Sea* restored his reputation and earned Hemingway the Pulitzer Prize in 1953. In 1954, Hemingway won the Nobel

Prize for Literature. The prize committee cited the power of his style, his mastery of narration, and his admiration for the individual who "fights the good fight" in a "world of reality overshadowed by violence and death."

In 1959, Hemingway bought a home in Ketchum, Idaho. In declining health from diabetes, high blood pressure, and mental depression (possibly caused by a genetic illness unrecognized at the time), he attended the Spanish bullfights in 1960 and later celebrated his 60th birthday. At the Mayo Clinic, he twice underwent electric shock treatments, which didn't help him. So great was Hemingway's stature as both a writer and legendary figure, the world mourned after his suicide by shotgun at his home in Ketchum on July 2, 1961.

A number of Hemingway's works were published posthumously. *A Moveable Feast*, published in 1964, contains striking and sometimes abusive representations of the famous literary figures Hemingway had known in Paris. *Islands in the Stream*, published in 1970, is a semi-autobiographical novel, set in the Caribbean, about a painter, his relationships with his family, his loneliness, and his violent death. *The Dangerous Summer*, published in 1985, is based on a bullfight "duel" Hemingway witnessed in Spain in 1960. *The Garden of Eden*, published in 1986, recounts the love affairs of two women and one man, explores complex gender issues, and has prompted many critics to reconsider earlier assessments of Hemingway's machismo.

While Hemingway the dedicated writer and careful editor may seem somewhat at odds with Hemingway the legendary man of action, both sides contributed to a lasting literary legacy. As the dominant concerns of successive generations have changed, readers from each generation have found new understanding and appreciation of Hemingway's works. For example, the generation of Baby Boomers profoundly affected by the Vietnam War found much to identify with in the lost generation's alienation in *The Sun Also Rises*. Subsequent generations, increasingly concerned with international economics and threats to the global environment, may well find the multicultural aspects of Hemingway's literature irresistible and appreciate more fully the environmental foresight of works like *The Old Man and the Sea*. And as the World War II generation (like the World War I generation before it) passes away, Hemingway's works will remain an invaluable contribution to twentieth-century literature and to the historical perspective of future generations.

INTRODUCTION TO THE NOVELLA

The following Introduction section is provided solely as an educational tool and is not meant to replace the experience of your reading the work. Read the Introduction and A Brief Synopsis to enhance your understanding of the work and to prepare yourself for the critical thinking that should take place whenever you read any work of fiction or nonfiction. Keep the List of Characters and Character Map at hand so that as you read the original literary work, if you encounter a character about whom you're uncertain, you can refer to the List of Characters and Character Map to refresh your memory.

Introduction

In April of 1936, Hemingway published an essay in *Esquire* magazine entitled "On the Blue Water: A Gulf Stream Letter," which contained a paragraph about an old man who went fishing alone in a skiff far out at sea, landed a huge marlin, and then lost much of it to sharks. As early as 1939, the year he moved to Cuba, Hemingway began planning an expansion of this kernel into a fully developed story that would become part of a larger volume. (Indeed, other sections of that proposed volume were published after his death as part of *Islands in the Stream*.)

Early in 1951, Hemingway finally began writing *The Old Man and the Sea* at his home near Havana. The government of Cuban President Carlos Prio Socarras was in decline and would eventually be overthrown in 1952 by U.S.-supported dictator Fulgencio Batista, who in turn would be ousted in 1959 by Fidel Castro. The Soviet Union had detonated an atomic bomb in late 1949. The United States, under the Truman administration, advanced a policy designed to contain Soviet expansionism; supported such international actions as the formation of the United Nations, the Truman Doctrine of 1947, and the Marshall Plan of 1948; and became embroiled in the Korean War. Senator Joseph R. McCarthy initiated a Red Scare paranoia in his four-year search for communist sympathizers. And the booming U.S. population and postwar economy fueled American consumption. Although *The Old Man and the Sea* takes place in September of 1950, it exists outside (or just at the edge) of these and other significant events of the period.

However, the novella does reflect a universal pattern of socioeconomic change familiar even today among developing nations. In rural Cuba of the 1930s and 1940s, the traditional fishing culture (insulated and isolated from the industrialized world, closely connected to nature, bereft of modern technology, and bound to extended families and tightly knit communities) began shifting to the material progress of a fishing industry (dependent on the industrialized world for its livelihood, environmentally oblivious or negligent, increasingly reliant on mechanized methods to ensure profit, and much less bound to extended families and local communities). In *The Old Man and the Sea*, Hemingway depicts Santiago as a dedicated fisherman whose craft is integral to his own identity, his code of behavior, and nature's order. On the other hand, Hemingway portrays the pragmatic younger fishermen as those who supply shark livers for the cod liver oil industry in the United States, use their profits to purchase motorized boats and other mechanized equipment, and approach their fishing strictly as a means to improve their material circumstances.

Similarly, Santiago's personal history represents something of universal journey, as critics such as Angel Capellán and Bickford Sylvester have pointed out. Santiago is culturally a Spaniard and therefore a European. As a native of the Canary Islands, who made frequent trips to the coast of Africa, he also embodies something of Africa. And as an émigré to Cuba, a journey made by many Spaniards from Europe, he is both a Cuban (symbolized by the image on his wall of the patroness of Cuba, the Virgin of Cobre) and an American. Santiago has brought with him to the New World some Old World European and African values of dedication to craft and acceptance of one's role in the natural order and joined those to a decidedly American preoccupation with living one's life according to an independent and individual code of behavior that redeems the individual's existence.

The novella is truly universal in its consideration of the plight of an old man struggling against age, poverty, loneliness, and mortality to maintain his identity and dignity, reestablish his reputation in the community, and ensure for all time his relationship with those he loves and to whom he hopes to pass on everything he values most. Ultimately, Santiago's heroic struggle not only redeems himself but inspires and spiritually enriches those around him.

After the critical disapproval that met his previous novel, *Across the River and Into the Trees* (1950), a symbolic love story and meditation on war in modern times, Hemingway, like Santiago, needed a big success to reestablish his reputation. He first published *The Old Man and the Sea* in its entirety in *Life* magazine in 1952. The novella subsequently became a Book-of-the-Month-Club selection and a best seller. It gained immediate critical acclaim and earned Hemingway the Pulitzer Prize in 1953 and the American Academy of Arts and Letters' Award of Merit Medal for the Novel. It also contributed to his receiving the Nobel Prize for Literature in 1954. In 1958, the novella became a movie starring Spencer Tracy.

A Brief Synopsis

For 84 days, the old fisherman Santiago has caught nothing. Alone, impoverished, and facing his own mortality, Santiago is now considered unlucky. So Manolin (Santiago's fishing partner until recently and the young man Santiago has taught since the age of five) has been constrained by his parents to fish in another, more productive boat. Every evening, though, when Santiago again returns empty-handed, Manolin helps carry home the old man's equipment, keeps him company, and brings him food.

On the morning of the 85th day, Santiago sets out before dawn on a three-day odyssey that takes him far out to sea. In search of an epic catch, he eventually does snag a marlin of epic proportions, enduring tremendous hardship to land the great fish. He straps the marlin along the length of his skiff and heads for home, hardly believing his own victory. Within an hour, a mako shark attacks the marlin, tearing away a great hunk of its flesh and mutilating Santiago's prize. Santiago fights the mako, enduring great suffering, and eventually kills it with his harpoon, which he loses in the struggle.

The great tear in the marlin's flesh releases the fish's blood and scent into the water, attracting packs of shovel-nosed sharks. With whatever equipment remains on board, Santiago repeatedly fights off the packs of these scavengers, enduring exhaustion and great physical pain, even tearing something in his chest. Eventually, the sharks pick the marlin clean. Defeated, Santiago reaches shore and beaches the skiff. Alone in the dark, he looks back at the marlin's skeleton in the reflection from a street light and then stumbles home to his shack, falling face down onto his cot in exhaustion.

The next morning, Manolin finds Santiago in his hut and cries over the old man's injuries. Manolin fetches coffee and hears from the other fisherman what he had already seen—that the marlin's skeleton lashed to the skiff is eighteen feet long, the greatest fish the village has known. Manolin sits with Santiago until he awakes and then gives the old man some coffee. The old man tells Manolin that he was beaten. But Manolin reassures him that the great fish didn't beat him and that they will fish together again, that luck doesn't matter, and that the old man still has much to teach him.

That afternoon, some tourists see the marlin's skeleton waiting to go out with the tide and ask a waiter what it is. Trying to explain what happened to the marlin, the waiter replies, "Eshark." But the tourists misunderstand and assume that's what the skeleton is.

Back in his shack, with Manolin sitting beside him, Santiago sleeps again and dreams of the young lions he had seen along the coast of Africa when he was a young man.

List of Characters

Santiago   The novella's central character. A dedicated fisherman who taught Manolin everything he knows about fishing, Santiago is now old and poor and has gone 84 days without a catch.

Manolin   A young man from the fishing village who has fished with Santiago since the age of five and now cares for the old man. Manolin recently began fishing with another fisherman whom his parents consider luckier than Santiago.

Martin   The owner of the Terrace (his name is Spanish for St. Martin), he sends food and drink to Santiago through Manolin.

Rogelio   A man of the village who on occasion helps Santiago with the fishing net.

Perico   A man at the *bodega* (his name is Spanish for St. Peter, an apostle and fisherman) who gives Santiago newspapers to read.

Marlin   An eighteen-foot bluish billfish and a catch of legendary proportions.

Mako   A mackerel shark (*dentuso* in Spanish) that is a voracious and frightening killer known for its rows of large, sharp teeth.

Shovel-nosed sharks   The scavenger sharks (*galanos* in Spanish) that destroy the marlin.

Pedrico   A fisherman in the village who looks after Santiago's skiff and gear and receives the marlin's head to use in fish traps.

Tourists   A man and woman at the Terrace who see the marlin's skeleton and, misunderstanding a waiter's explanation of what happened, think the skeleton is that of a shark.

Character Map

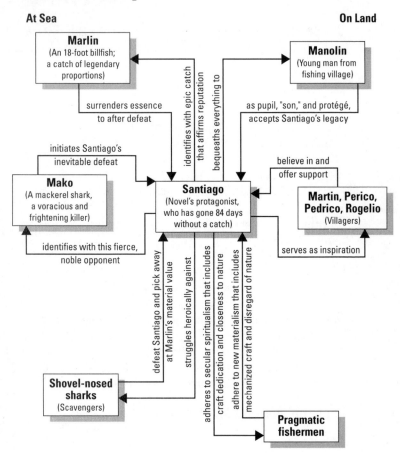

At Sea

On Land

Marlin
(An 18-foot billfish; a catch of legendary proportions)

Manolin
(Young man from fishing village)

surrenders essence to after defeat

identifies with epic catch that affirms reputation

bequeaths everything to

as pupil, "son," and protégé, accepts Santiago's legacy

initiates Santiago's inevitable defeat

believe in and offer support

Mako
(A mackerel shark, a voracious and frightening killer)

Santiago
(Novel's protagonist, who has gone 84 days without a catch)

Martin, Perico, Pedrico, Rogelio
(Villagers)

identifies with this fierce, noble opponent

serves as inspiration

defeat Santiago and pick away at Marlin's material value

struggles heroically against

adheres to secular spiritualism that includes craft dedication and closeness to nature

adhere to new materialism that includes mechanized craft and disregard of nature

Shovel-nosed sharks
(Scavengers)

Pragmatic fishermen

CRITICAL COMMENTARIES

The sections that follow provide great tools for supplementing your reading of *The Old Man and the Sea*. First, in order to enhance your understanding of and enjoyment from reading, we provide quick summaries in case you have difficulty when you read the original literary work. Each summary is followed by commentary: literary devices, character analyses, themes, and so on. Keep in mind that the interpretations here are solely those of the author of this study guide and are used to jumpstart your thinking about the work. No single interpretation of a complex work like *The Old Man and the Sea* is infallible or exhaustive, and you'll likely find that you interpret portions of the work differently from the author of this study guide. Read the original work and determine your own interpretations, referring to these Notes for supplemental meanings only.

Part One
Preparations

Summary

For 84 days, the old fisherman Santiago has caught nothing, return-ing empty-handed in his skiff to the small Cuban fishing village where he lives. After 40 days without a catch, Manolin's father has insisted that Manolin, the young man Santiago taught to fish from the age of five, fish in another boat.

This evening, as every evening, Manolin meets the old man to help carry the coiled line, gaff, harpoon, and sail back to his shack. Along the way, Manolin tries to cheer Santiago by reminding him of the time, when they were fishing together, that the old man went 87 days with-out a fish and then they caught big fish for three weeks.

On their way home, Manolin buys Santiago a beer at the Terrace. Some of the other fishermen make fun of Santiago; others look at him and are sad, speaking politely about the current and the depths at which they had fished and what they had seen at sea. The fishermen who were successful this day have taken their marlin to the fish house or their sharks to the shark factory. Manolin asks if he can get sardines for San-tiago tomorrow. Santiago at first tells him to go play baseball but even-tually relents. They reminisce a while, talk of Santiago's plans for going out the next day, and then go to Santiago's shack. Because Santiago has nothing to eat, Manolin fetches Santiago the dinner that the Terrace owner, Martin, sends for free, as he has many times before. As Santi-ago eats, he and the boy talk of baseball, the great Joe DiMaggio, and other topics of mutual interest.

The next morning, Santiago picks up the boy at his house. They have coffee (which is all that Santiago will have all day) at an early morn-ing spot that serves fishermen. The boy fetches sardines and fresh bait and helps the old man ease his skiff into the water. They wish each other good luck, and the old man rows away.

Commentary

The first quarter of this novella takes place on land, in a small Cuban fishing village on Tuesday evening, September 12, and Wednesday morning, September 13, 1950. The novella's point-of view in this section is that of an *omniscient narrator* (in the sense of knowing more than any one character and having access to the perspectives of multiple characters). With the exception of minor shifting to Manolin's thoughts, this third-person narrative is limited to and concentrates on Santiago and his actions. What readers know of Santiago's thoughts in this section of the novella comes from the narrator's statement of them, although this perspective later shifts when the story shifts to the sea. Most of this section's activities represent the characters' preparations for Santiago's setting out to sea on Wednesday morning for what will become the story's great struggle. Yet almost immediately those activities become surface realism, details that are mentioned but mostly glossed over and seen as the routine Santiago usually follows. On the other hand, Hemingway's preparations here not only set the stage but predict the plot of this deceptively simple tale, touch on the story's multiple themes, and begin to reveal in the story and its characters layers of meaning and larger and larger significances.

Literary Device

From its first paragraphs, the novella is replete with religious images and allusions. After 40 days without a catch in Santiago's boat, Manolin's parents have sent him out with another fisherman because they believe that Santiago is unlucky. The number 40 here suggests the stories of Noah (who also had to endure social separateness and ridicule and endure great hardship on a boat at sea) and of Moses (who was able to see the Promised Land and lead the children of Israel to it but never dwell there himself). Likewise, Manolin's catch of three fish his first day out with the other fisherman suggests the three days the people of Israel went without water before Moses struck the rock, the Trinity, and the story of the loaves and fishes that fed the multitude of Christ's followers. Santiago's name is Spanish for St. James, an apostle and fisherman. Men who are kind to Santiago are named Perico and Pedrico (both forms for Saint Peter) and Martin (for Saint Martin), suggesting disciples, spiritual followers, or men of faith. On the wall of Santiago's shack hangs a portrait of the Virgin of Cobre, the patroness of Cuba. Even Manolin's name (the diminutive of Manuel) is Spanish for Emmanuel, the Redeemer, although the full significance of his name becomes clear only at the story's end.

While entirely appropriate to Cuba's pervasively Catholic culture, these images and allusions suggest far more than any sectarian or even broadly religious dogma (as many critics, including Arvin Wells and Philip Young, have mentioned). These images and allusions run parallel to other images and allusions just as appropriate to Cuba's culture—such as a passion for baseball (its heroics and statistics) and an enthusiasm for games of chance (such as the lottery). These images and allusions span the secular to the profane and yoke religious conviction to a palpable belief in luck, which is also mentioned in the first paragraph.

For example, one of the places in which Hemingway yokes religion and baseball occurs when Santiago tells Manolin that the Yankees must have won their game, and Manolin expresses his fear that the Yankees will be beaten by another team. Their discussion follows the formal ritual of religious instruction, and indeed Santiago uses the discussion to remind Manolin to have faith and resist fear: "Be careful or you will fear even the Reds of Cincinnati and the White Sox of Chicago." Because the Reds play in the National League, not the American League in which the Yankees play, Santiago's chiding is a reminder of the irrationality of fear, which can rob one of the power faith confers.

Theme

This yoking is neither derogatory nor blasphemous. Like religion, baseball and games of chance rely on ritual and have the power to engender hope, dreams, faith, absorption, and resolution (so integral to this story)—ultimately taking people beyond themselves. Together, these images and allusions suggest a theme of transformation and a larger spiritual dimension possible in the human condition: Human beings can summon imaginative vision, as well as physical endurance, creating the capacity to withstand and even transcend hardships.

Literary Device

That central theme radiates beyond the surface realism in this very human tale of an impoverished old man, his love for a young man who also loves him, and his trials in bringing in a big fish. Certainly that story is central, and Hemingway the journalist would have nothing less. Still, the theme's possibilities also push this tale toward *allegory*—a story with a surface meaning and one or more under-the-surface meanings; a narrative form so ancient and natural to the human mind as to be universal; a form used in pagan mythology, in both Testaments of the Bible, and in Classical to Post-Modern literature. In short, the novella invites, even demands, reading on multiple levels.

Hemingway's early descriptions of Santiago support the central theme and *foreshadow* (predict) the novella's ostensibly simple yet artfully designed plot. The old man's shirt, like his sail, is patched beyond all recognition. He is thin and gaunt, from a long life of hard work and times with little to eat. He has deep wrinkles on the back of his neck and blotches of skin cancer on his face and hands from a life spent in the sun's reflection on the tropical sea. His hands are scarred from handling heavy fish on cords, but the scars are "old as erosions in a fishless desert." Here is a poor man whose best days are behind him; who never had children; whose wife has died; who has known fishless stretches without the catch upon which his meager existence, the community's respect, and his sense of identity as an accomplished fisherman all depend. Job-like in his hardships, Santiago is a man who has endured many ordeals.

Clearly, Santiago is the next iteration in a long line of Hemingway's literary heroes: a man of action, tested by adversity, who lives by his own beliefs. When Manolin observes that Santiago's eyes (unlike those of the man whom Manolin now fishes with) are still good, Santiago describes himself as "a strange old man." He is *strange* in the sense that he is unconventional in his society. He remains dedicated to his principles (his own internal code of behavior) and to his passion for his profession above concerns for material gain or survival. Yet even for a Hemingway hero, Santiago is something special. After Manolin presses Santiago to accept some fresh baits, Santiago (who is also somewhat reminiscent of Don Quixote) proffers his customary protests to save face but eventually agrees: "'_Thank you,' the old man said. He was too simple to wonder when he had attained humility. But he knew he had attained it and he knew it was not disgraceful and it carried no loss of true pride."

Character Insight

Here, too, is a man who still has powerful shoulders, whose eyes are not old but the color of the sea and "cheerful and undefeated," who knows "many tricks" and has "resolution." Santiago's strength and his vision are not that of an old man. His eyes remain cheerful and undefeated because one of the many "tricks" he has learned—arguably more vital than his tricks of the fisherman's craft—is the transcendent power of imaginative vision. Whether drawing his inspiration and confidence from religion, baseball, games of chance, memories of his own youth, his love for Manolin, or something else, Santiago knows how to keep alive in himself and others the hope, dreams, faith, absorption, and resolution essential to withstand suffering, transcend it, and ultimately transform one's self.

Just as this realistic story tends toward allegory, Santiago and Manolin, as specific individuals, also can be seen as *archetypal* characters (universal representations inherited from the collective consciousness of our ancestors and the fundamental facts of human existence). Santiago is mentor, spiritual father, and the old man (*viejo* in Spanish) or old age; Manolin is pupil, son, and the boy (*chico* in Spanish) or youth. Many of their conversations have an element of ritual (such as the little fictions they engage in to preserve the old man's dignity—the food he says he has in his house, their talk of using the cast net they both know Santiago had to sell, their talk of borrowing some money for a lottery ticket, and so forth). Their conversations also have the rhythm and structure of a catechism or religious instruction. Manolin is Santiago's last and deepest human relationship; his replacement in the natural order; the one to whom he wishes to entrust his skill as a fisherman, the transforming power of his vision, and his memory.

That is why, when he is asleep, Santiago no longer dreams "of storms, nor of women, nor of great occurrences, nor of great fish, nor fights, nor contests of strength, nor of his wife." For the most part, life's challenges and adventures are no longer his. He never dreams about Manolin, because the boy is part of a future Santiago can never know. Instead, Santiago dreams of young lions on the beach in Africa, where he sailed as a young man about Manolin's current age. Santiago loves the young lions as he loves "the boy"—meaning both the young man Santiago himself was and the young man Manolin is now.

Conventionally regarded as kings of the animal world, the young lions *symbolize* (represent) qualities such as courage, strength, grace, dignity—in short, all the qualities of a champion that Santiago holds dear in his own youthful memories and would bequeath to Manolin. Here is age bequeathing to youth whatever pieces of the species' collective knowledge age possesses. Here, too, is age recalling its own youth and reliving that youth vicariously in the vigor of the young. In this commingling of Santiago's youthful reminiscences with his hopes for Manolin, the lions also suggest Santiago's immortality. Confronted with life's natural cycle from youth to old age, the only immortality is in whatever one leaves the young.

While the writing in the novella is a tour-de-force, Hemingway's effort to pare down language and convey as much as possible in as few words as possible, the meanings here resonate on a larger and larger scale, as if ripples in water after a fish jump. For example, Hemingway conveys the novella's central theme in more ways than in the yoking of religious conviction with a belief in luck. Relying on a technique also used by T. S. Eliot and James Joyce, Hemingway the journalist enriches the story and advances its themes with resonances from historical, factual references. Having read yesterday's newspaper, the old man tells the boy about "the baseball" (*el beisbol* in Spanish):

> "In the American League it is the Yankees as I said," the old man said happily.
>
> "They lost today," the boy told him.
>
> "That means nothing. The great DiMaggio is himself again."

Not only does the reference to DiMaggio reflect Santiago's deep faith and predict his upcoming battle at sea in the "month when the great fish come," but critics (including C. Harold Hurley and Bickford Sylvester) also have researched such references to determine the exact dates in September when the story takes place. From these dates can be inferred a great deal about Cuba's cultural, economic, and social circumstances in this story.

Critics also have established Manolin's exact age as 22, based on his reference to the baseball player Dick Sisler. "The great Sisler's father was never poor and he, the father, was playing in the Big Leagues when he was my age." Clearly, Manolin is a young man, referred to as "the boy" in this story from the old man's affectionate perspective and the Hispanic custom of referring to an unmarried man this way. Manolin is no child, but an apprentice, disciple, or initiate preparing to carry on, in Santiago's place, his most precious skills and beliefs. At the same time, both Manolin and Santiago recognize that Manolin is subject to the authority of his parents. Santiago tells Manolin, "If you were my boy I'd take you out and gamble . . . but you are your father's and your mother's and you are in a lucky boat."

Early on, Hemingway expands the central theme by introducing supporting themes such as those suggested in a brief mention of the fish house and the shark factory:

> The successful fishermen of that day were already in and had butchered their marlin out and carried them laid full length across two planks, with two men staggering at the end of each plank, to the fish house where they waited for the ice truck to carry them to the market in Havana.

> Those who had caught sharks had taken them to the shark factory on the other side of the cove where they were hoisted on a block and tackle, their livers removed, their fins cut off and their hides skinned out and their flesh cut into strips for salting.
>
> When the wind was in the east a smell came across the harbour from the shark factory; but today there was only the faint edge of the odour because the wind had backed into the north and then dropped off. . . .

Theme

Not only does the description of what becomes of the marlin and the sharks foreshadow Santiago's battles, but it also suggests another variation on the theme of the natural order and man's role in it. As Santiago's relationship with Manolin suggests the natural cycle of life from youth to old age, this description suggests that all living beings can be viewed as both predator and prey. In that view, fishermen like Santiago, dedicated to their vocation and relying on their skill for their living, are part of the natural order.

Set against that view, the description of the fish house and the shark factory also suggests Cuba's changing socioeconomic circumstances (a smell coming from the north) and a village fishing culture converting to an exploitive fishing industry, as many critics, including Bickford Sylvester, have mentioned. This situation creates conflict between the new and the old economies, between the mechanical fishermen motivated by money and the passionate, skill-conscious fishermen dedicated to a vocation they see as a part of nature's cycle and a more spiritual way of life.

Viewed in this light, Manolin's father (who "hasn't much faith" and so insists Manolin fish in a more productive boat), the "almost blind" man Manolin now fishes with, and the young fishermen who ridicule Santiago at the Terrace are all pragmatic, practical men devoted to what they see as progress in this new materialism. On the other hand, Santiago, Manolin, the old fishermen who treat Santiago with respect, and the village shopkeepers who give him food or a newspaper or other small tokens of support are all idealists devoted to something enlarging in the old ways, something that nourishes the human spirit, something beyond material gain.

Glossary

(Here and in the following glossary sections, difficult words and phrases, as well as allusions and historical references are explained.)

gaff   a large, strong hook on a pole, or a barbed spear, used in landing large fish.

marlin   any of several large, slender, deep-sea billfishes.

Dick Sisler   famous baseball player and coach on numerous baseball teams, including the Cardinals, the Reds, and the Yankees.

Joe DiMaggio   famous baseball player who played for the Yankees and is widely regarded as the best all-around player in baseball history.

John J. McGraw   manager of the Giants from 1902 to 1932.

Leo Durocher   manager of the Brooklyn Dodgers from 1939 to 1946 and 1948.

Adolpho Luque   pitcher for the Reds and Giants and a native of Havana, Cuba.

Mike Gonzalez   catcher for the Cardinals (1916–1918, 1924) and a native of Cuba.

Que va   (Spanish) No way.

oakum   loose, stringy hemp fiber gotten by taking apart old ropes and treated with tar, used as a caulking material.

Mosquito Coast   region on the Caribbean coast of Honduras and Nicaragua.

Canary Islands   group of islands in the Atlantic, off northwest Africa, forming a region of Spain.

Virgin of Cobre   reference to the statue of Our Lady of La Caridad de Cobre (Our Lady of Charity at Cobre), the most venerated in all of Cuba.

Part Two
The Journey Out

Summary

Alone in his boat, in the dark of early morning, Santiago rows out to sea. He hears the other fishermen leaving in their boats but cannot see them in the dark. He passes the phosphorescence of some Gulf weed and one of the deep wells where many fish and other sea creatures congregate. He has fished such deep wells without success on previous days of this long stretch without a catch. So this day, he plans to row far out to sea, in search of a really big fish.

As he rows, Santiago hears the flying fish he regards as friends and feels sympathy for the delicate sea birds that must fish to survive and must cope with an ocean that can be beautiful yet cruel. He also thinks about the differences between himself and the younger fishermen who float their lines on buoys and use motorboats bought with money they earned selling shark livers. Whereas Santiago affectionately refers to the sea as *la mar* (using the Spanish feminine), they say *el mar* (using the Spanish masculine).

Santiago rows effortlessly, not disturbing the ocean's surface but working with the current, letting it do a third of the work. He sets his baits at precise depths and ties and sews them so that all the hook is concealed and sweet smelling and good tasting to a fish. He uses the albacores Manolin bought for him and a big blue runner and a yellow jack he had from before, using the sardines to give them scent and attractiveness. He loops each line onto a green-sapped stick, so that even a touch on the bait will make the stick dip, and connects the coils of line so that a fish can run out more than 300 fathoms if necessary.

As he fishes, Santiago takes pride in keeping his lines straighter than anyone, even though he knows that other fishermen sometimes let their lines drift with the current. For a moment, he reluctantly admits that, despite his precision, he has no luck anymore. But he quickly reminds himself that each day is a new day and that, while it is better to be lucky, he prefers to be exact so that he will be ready when the luck finally comes. Santiago briefly reflects that all his life the early morning sun has hurt his eyes, yet again catches himself, keeping in mind that his eyes are still good and in the evening he can look into the sun without getting the blackness.

Santiago sees a man-of-war bird circling in the sky ahead of him. Through his experience and his fisherman's skill, he recognizes that the bird is following a school of flying fish, themselves pursued by a school of big dolphin. Santiago works with nature, fishing where the bird leads, but neither he nor the bird have any luck. As the flying fish (which have little chance against the dolphin) move too fast for the bird, the school of dolphin move too fast and too far for Santiago. Santiago clings to the hope that perhaps he will catch a stray, but the dolphin get away.

Santiago studies a Portuguese man-of-war (*agua mala* he calls it in Spanish) floating in the water. He notices the tiny fish swimming in its filaments and notes that while these fish are immune to its poisons, men are not. While working on a fish, he has many times suffered welts and sores from the poisons. He considers the man-of-war's iridescent beauty the falsest thing in the sea, and he thinks how much he loves to watch sea turtles eat them or to step on them himself on the beach after a storm.

Santiago recalls his days turtling and thinks that "people are heartless about turtles because a turtle's heart will beat for hours after he has been cut up and butchered." He muses that his heart is like the turtle's, as are his hands and feet, and that he eats turtle eggs to be strong in the fall when the big fish come, the same reason he drinks the shark liver oil available in the shack where the fishermen store their equipment. Although the oil is there for anyone who wants it, most of the fishermen don't like it. But Santiago considers it no worse than the early hours fishermen keep, and he drinks it because it gives him strength, is good for the eyes, and protects against colds and grippes.

The second time Santiago sees the bird circling above him, he sees tuna jumping into the air. Santiago successfully catches a ten-pound albacore and hauls it into the boat, where it flops around until he kills it out of kindness. Santiago says aloud that the fish will make a good bait, which prompts him to begin thinking about his habit of talking aloud to himself at sea, a habit that he began after Manolin stopped fishing with him. He remembers that he and Manolin talked only when necessary or at night when bad weather had them storm-bound. Most fishermen consider talking only when necessary at sea a virtue, and Santiago has always respected that belief. Now, however, he grants himself this minor indiscretion because it bothers no one. He knows that if the others hear him, they will consider him crazy, but he decides that if he is crazy, this habit doesn't matter and that the rich take along their radios to listen to baseball games.

Santiago upbraids himself for thinking of baseball when he should be focusing his attention on what he describes as "[t]hat which I was born for." He shifts his thoughts to something he has observed this day—all the fish he has seen are moving fast, travelling to the northeast. Although he is not sure whether that is a sign of bad weather or something else, he has noticed. He also notices that he is now so far out into the ocean that he can barely see the tops of the tallest hills, which look white in the distance. With the sun hot on his back, Santiago briefly is tempted to nap, with a line around his toe to wake him if a fish bites. But he remembers that he has been trying to catch a fish for 85 days now and so "must fish the day well." At that moment, one of the green sticks take a sharp dip.

Commentary

The novella's overall structure can be divided, according to setting, into three parts—the three phases of Santiago's cyclical journey from the land to the sea and then back to the land again. (This cyclical journey also suggests the cyclical quality of human life and the various cycles of the natural world, such as the change of season or the interdependency of all living creatures in the food chain.) The novella's middle part, which takes place at sea, actually comprises the bulk of the story, its central action, and its most dramatic moments. However, by considering first what takes place on Santiago's voyage out and then what takes place during his great sea battles, special attention can be focused on the first section's realistic description and other details that should not be glossed over lightly.

Literary Device

As Santiago, alone in his boat, rows out to sea, the third-person, omniscient narrative of the first part on land begins to shift a bit and continues to do so throughout the second part at sea. Here the perspective draws closer to Santiago, entering his mind with increasing regularity as Hemingway begins blending *narrative modes* (methods of telling the story). Sometimes this movement into Santiago's thoughts is signaled traditionally, with a tag such as *he thought* or with *he said* and the conventional quotation marks around what Santiago actually speaks aloud. (Attention is even paid to this handy literary device in

Santiago's explanation that he permits himself to talk aloud while at sea without Manolin.) At other times, the narrative drifts almost imperceptibly into Santiago's thoughts (sometimes cast as first-person interior monologue) or the quotation marks around whatever Santiago speaks aloud to himself eventually disappear.

Although only about half the length of the novella's previous part on land, this first section of the much lengthier part at sea adds much more than a simple build up of suspense. Here Hemingway begins to demonstrate Santiago's considerable skill as a fisherman (gained through a lifetime of experience), his dedication to his vocation, and his capacity to cultivate and draw upon the inspiration and imaginative vision he needs to sustain himself in the face of hardship. Here we see that Santiago, even with his better days behind him, is still a man in charge, still an expert who knows what to do and knows the tricks of his fisherman's craft. He is also still a man whose imaginative vision remains strong despite a lifetime of hardships that have hurt him, as the morning sun has always hurt his eyes.

In this section, Hemingway also dramatizes Santiago's relationship to the natural world and his place in the natural order, a place all fishermen like Santiago assume. Hemingway also begins to demonstrate Santiago's philosophy in action and to distinguish for the reader Santiago's code of behavior from that of the fishermen who are not like him. In short, the descriptive details and other information Hemingway provides in this section resonate with the novella's ever-expanding meanings.

With every "thrust of the blades in the water," Santiago cuts himself off from the land and the human community ashore: "The old man knew he was going far out and he left the smell of the land behind and rowed out into the clean early morning smell of the ocean." Putting the humiliation of his life ashore behind him, leaving behind the young man he loves, Santiago begins his solitary quest for the big fish that will once again affirm his identity as a great fisherman, restore the respect of his community, and solidify his relationship with Manolin in a way that will last beyond his death.

Setting out to sea, Santiago resembles something of Homer's Odysseus setting forth or Cervantes' Don Quixote commencing a noble quest (as many critics, including Angel Capellán and Sergio H. Bocaz, have mentioned). Yet Santiago, alone in the dark, is neither seeking adventure and material gain like Odysseus, nor is he self-deluded like Don Quixote. Santiago instead becomes a solitary human representative to the natural world, which is larger than human society, and a participant in the natural order of predator and prey that binds all life together in complete interdependency.

Style & Language

Amid such resonances, Hemingway the journalist immediately anchors the story in the realistic details of ocean life—the seaweed, the creatures that inhabit the deep wells, the flying fish. Hemingway actually even evokes the sound the flying fish make with the repeated sibilant *s* in his description of "the hissing that their stiff set wings made as they soared away in the darkness." With that sound of the flying fish, the narrative moves inside Santiago's thoughts. He recognizes that the flying fish are his friends. He also empathizes with the sea birds, who share so much of his own hardship in their "flying and looking and almost never finding," and he thinks that "the birds have a harder life than we do."

Theme

Out of these musings comes a philosophical question that echoes Job's question to God about why the good are made to suffer: "Why did they make birds so delicate and fine as those sea swallows when the ocean can be so cruel?" Like Job, Santiago receives no satisfactory answer that he can understand, simply an ongoing recognition that he and all of nature's creatures participate in the same pattern of necessity. He shares an affectionate kinship with all living creatures that must prey upon and be preyed upon in turn, for all share and are subject to the same conditions of life.

Presented here so concisely is something of the philosophical basis for the behavioral code of fishermen like Santiago, who respect nature and see themselves as part of it, relying upon their skill and dedication to their craft to participate in nature's eternal pattern. By extension of this philosophy, Santiago affectionately refers to the sea, which is so beautiful, as *la mar* (the Spanish feminine) and loves her even as he recognizes that she is part of nature and so cannot help her occasional cruelty.

Hemingway demonstrates this philosophy in action by conveying the details of Santiago's considerable skill as a fisherman and of the precision with which he performs each task, as though it were religious ritual. For example, by rowing steadily, keeping within his speed, not disturbing the ocean's surface, and "letting the current do a third of the work," Santiago discovers at first light that "he was already further out than he had hoped to be at this hour." Twice he follows a circling bird, recognizing it as a clear sign of where to fish. Exercising great care in the way he baits his hooks, he ensures that there is "no part of the hook that a great fish could feel which was not sweet smelling and good tasting." Santiago also keeps his lines "straighter than anyone did."

In direct contrast, and presented just as concisely, is something of the philosophical basis for the behavior of the mechanized fishermen who "used buoys as floats for their lines and had motorboats, bought when the shark livers had brought much money." These pragmatic, practical materialists refer to the sea as *el mar* (the Spanish masculine) and speak of the sea as "a contestant or a place or even an enemy." As they play out their philosophical position, they sow the seeds of their own economic destruction in the future ravages of long-line fishing, powerful motorboats, and other environmental disregard (as critics such as Bickford Sylvester have observed).

As Santiago muses about his precision in keeping his lines straight while others "let them drift with the current," he is also forced to admit that he has no luck. This recognition that sometimes the unworthy prosper expands upon his earlier Job-like question. Yet Santiago quickly reestablishes his faith in his own skill, its philosophical basis, and the hope of each new day. Here again Hemingway yokes religious conviction and a belief in luck through the possibility that both confer. Santiago's faith sustains him and offers him hope so that he can endure and remain strong even in the face of 84 days without a catch, old age, poverty, loneliness, social separateness, mortality, and so on.

Theme

Indeed, embedded within Santiago's hope that if one is exact one will be ready when the luck comes is the echo of an old aphorism about God helping those who help themselves. While Benjamin Franklin said it of God, Aesop earlier said it of the gods. In both cases, the aphorism recognizes that in the face of unknowable and uncontrollable forces, one must rely on one's own abilities while keeping faith and hope alive. Almost immediately, Santiago also recognizes that despite the early sun that has hurt his eyes all his life, his eyes are still good. Here again, the realistic detail about his eyes becomes a metaphor for the inspiration and imaginative vision that sustain him and permit him to endure life's hardships.

So when Santiago first follows the bird, which is following the flying fish, he comes to realize that, as the bird "has no chance" because the flying fish "are too big for him," the dolphin also have "gotten away from me" because they are "moving out too fast and too far." Still,

Santiago clings to the hope that perhaps he will yet catch his big fish. He thinks, "My big fish must be somewhere."

Character Insight

As Santiago must constantly struggle with external hardships, he also must constantly renew his own faith in himself. When he must admit that his efforts this time have failed, his musings turn a bit bleak. His closeness to, and identification with, nature do not blind him to nature's cruelty or falseness. In fact, much of what Santiago understands about morality is closely bound to nature, for he sees the two coexist. For example, Santiago sees both cruelty and falseness in the beautiful iridescence of the Portuguese men-of-war, which sting the arms and hands of fishermen working their lines and cause sores much like poison ivy. For that reason, Santiago enjoys watching the turtles eat them or stepping on them when he walks on the beach. He also thinks about how most people "are heartless about turtles because a turtle's heart will beat for hours after he has been cut up and butchered." Santiago identifies with the turtles and, by extension, feels this same heartlessness directed toward himself, for he thinks, "I have such a heart too and my feet and hands are like theirs."

Yet Santiago's imaginative vision also enables him to find inspiration in this identification with the turtle and, by extension, all of nature, something ennobling that strengthens his faith in himself, his belief in possibility, and his will to endure. His thoughts turn to the white turtle eggs he always eats in the spring to give himself the strength to fish for the truly big fish in the fall. And he thinks of the foul-tasting shark liver oil that he drinks from a big drum in the fishermen's equipment shack, because the oil protects him from colds and grippes and is "good for the eyes."

Once again, Santiago affirms his place in the natural order and his kinship with all other living creatures as he reveals more of his tricks, not the least of which is his unfailing ability to endure. Once again, his "good eyes" represent the inspiration and imaginative vision that make possible his will to endure. As a result, the second time Santiago follows the circling bird, his skill, persistence, and faith yield a small reward in the ten-pound albacore he catches, a fish that will "make a beautiful bait."

Glossary

la mar, el mar   sea (Spanish feminine noun, Spanish masculine noun).

bonito   any of a genus of marine game and food scombroid fishes.

albacore   a tuna with unusually long pectoral fins, important as a game and food fish in all warm seas.

flying fish   a warm-sea fish with winglike pectoral fins that enable it to glide through the air.

big blue runner   any of various edible jack fishes of warm seas, as a bluish species and a striped bluish species.

yellow jack   an edible, gold-and-silver marine jack fish found near Florida and the West Indies.

dolphin   a game fish with colors that brighten and change when the fish is taken out of the water.

man-of-war bird   a large, tropical bird with extremely long wings and tail and a hooked beak.

plankton   the usually microscopic animal and plant life found floating or drifting in the ocean or in bodies of fresh water, used as food by nearly all aquatic animals.

Sargasso weed   floating brown algae found in tropical seas and having a main stem with flattened outgrowths like leaves, and branches with berry-like air sacs.

gelatinous   like gelatin or jelly; having the consistency of gelatin or jelly; viscous.

Portuguese man-of-war   a large, warm-sea jellyfish that floats on the water and has long, dangling tentacles with powerful stinging cells.

agua mala   (Spanish) jellyfish; Portuguese man-of-war.

carapace   the horny, protective covering over all or part of the back of certain animals, as the upper shell of the turtle, armadillo, crab, etc.

green turtle, hawk-bill, loggerhead   turtles.

Part Three
Battles at Sea: The Marlin and the Sharks

Summary

A sudden dip in one of the green sticks heralds the start of the novella's central battle. Holding the line gently between thumb and forefinger, Santiago somehow knows that a hundred fathoms down a great marlin is eating the sardines covering the hook that projects from the head of the small tuna. Santiago unleashes the line from the stick and lets the line run through his fingers, careful not to put any tension on it.

Santiago thinks about how big this fish must be, this far out and in this month, and desperately tries to coax or will the fish to eat the bait. He also asks God to help the fish to take the bait, and when the nibbling stops a couple of times, he desperately searches his experience for explanations that indicate the fish is still working on the bait. Then Santiago feels something hard and heavy and allows the line to play out, going deeper and deeper. He assumes the fish will turn and swallow the bait but is afraid to say so, out of a belief that "if you said a good thing it might not happen."

When he feels the fish eat the bait, he prepares the reserve coils of line, allows the fish to eat a bit more, and then sets the hook. He takes the weight of the taut line against his back, bracing himself against the boat and leaning back against the fish's pull on the line. For the first of many times during his great struggle, Santiago says fervently, "I wish I had the boy."

As the fish tows the boat, Santiago wonders what he'll do if the fish suddenly dives down deep and then dies. But he immediately assures himself that there are plenty of things he can do. He thinks about how he hooked the fish at noon and has been holding onto the line for four hours but hasn't yet had a first glimpse of the fish. Santiago drinks a bit of water from a bottle he has tucked away in the bow and tries not to think, but simply endure. When he realizes he can no longer see anything of the land, he reminds himself that he can always sail back by following the glow coming from Havana at night. Then he ponders various times when the fish might come up so he can see it.

After the sun goes down, Santiago ties the dried sack that had covered the bait box around his neck, so the sack hangs down his back and serves as a cushion under the fish line. In the dark, the line looks like a phosphorescent streak in the water. Then he checks the boat's course. Although the fish had been pulling the boat to the northwest, Santiago realizes that the current must be carrying them eastward now. He considers that if he loses the glare of Havana, then they must be going more eastward. Santiago briefly wonders about the results of the baseball game today and wishes he had a radio but then snaps himself up, scolding himself to keep his mind on what he's doing: "You must do nothing stupid." Again, Santiago says aloud, "I wish I had the boy. To help me and to see this." He thinks that, although no one should be alone in old age, it's unavoidable. Then he reminds himself to eat the tuna he caught earlier before it spoils, to keep himself strong.

When two porpoises come playing around the boat, Santiago speaks of them as "our brothers like the flying fish." Then he begins to pity the marlin, which is stronger and stranger than any fish he has ever hooked. Santiago considers whether the marlin has been hooked before, how the marlin cannot know that its adversary is only one old man, what price it may bring in the market, how it pulls like a male and without panic, and whether it has plans or is simply as desperate as he is.

Santiago remembers the time he hooked the female of a pair of marlins and the male stayed nearby until after Santiago had her in the boat. As Santiago was preparing the harpoon, the male jumped to see where the female was and then dove deep and was gone. Santiago still recalls the male marlin's beauty and how the whole incident was the saddest thing he ever saw. Both he and the boy felt sad afterwards, so they begged the female marlin's pardon and quickly butchered her.

Santiago thinks about the fact that both he and the marlin he has hooked have made a choice: the marlin's "to stay in the deep, dark water far out beyond all snares and traps and treacheries" and Santiago's "to go there to find him beyond all people." So now both are joined together, with no one to help either of them. At that moment, Santiago wonders whether he should not have been a fishermen, but then he reminds himself, "that was the thing that I was born for." Immediately, he snaps back to matters at hand, reminding himself to eat the tuna in the morning to keep up his strength.

In the night, Santiago catches another fish on one of his other lines but cuts it loose before he even knows what it is. He also cuts away the other leader line that is still in the water, so he can use all the reserve coils of line to bring in the marlin that he is joined in battle with. He abandons the other catch, the hooks, the lines, and the leaders to land this one fish. Santiago yearns for the boy but then yanks himself back to what he must do at the moment. When the marlin surges forward, the line cuts Santiago's face. He thinks that the fish's back cannot feel as bad as his does but that he has made all possible preparations and that the fish cannot pull the skiff forever. Santiago vows to stay with the fish until he's dead and then recognizes that the fish will do the same with him.

In the light of the second morning, the marlin and the current are still pulling the skiff to the north-northeast, but Santiago sees the fish is swimming at a shallower depth. He prays that God will let the fish jump, to fill the air sacs on its back so it cannot go deep and die, where he would lose it. Santiago keeps pulling the line taut, to the verge of breaking, each time worrying that the fish might throw the hook. He takes consolation that he feels better with the morning sun and that for once he doesn't have to look straight into it. Santiago tells the fish, "I love you and respect you very much. But I will kill you dead before this day ends." Then he thinks to himself, "Let us hope so."

A small, tired warbler flying south comes and sits on the line to rest. Santiago tells the bird the line is steady and then asks the bird what birds are coming to that it is so tired after a windless night. Then he thinks about the hawks the bird will have to face as it heads toward land and says, "Take a good rest, small bird. Then go in and take your chance like any man or bird or fish." He tells the bird that it can stay at his house, if it likes, and that he would take it in the boat if he weren't with "a friend," meaning the marlin. Then the marlin suddenly lurches, pulling Santiago into the bow. The bird flies up and is gone, and Santiago doesn't even see it go.

Santiago notices his bleeding right hand and speculates that something hurt the marlin at that moment and that the marlin is feeling the strain of all this now as he certainly is. He misses the bird's company and thinks that it is tougher where the bird is going, until it makes the shore. He thinks that he must have let his hand get cut by the line when the fish jumped because he's getting stupid or was distracted by the bird. So he vows to keep his mind on the task at hand, reminds himself to eat the tuna so his strength doesn't fail, and wishes for the boy again and for some salt. Santiago washes his hand in the salt water and with great care manages to position himself so he can eat the tuna. Santiago's left hand begins to cramp, and he disgustedly tells the hand to go ahead and turn into a claw, though it will do no good. As he eats the tuna, he hopes it will help his hand not to cramp.

Santiago wishes for some lime and salt for the fish but thinks that the taste is not bad anyway and preferable to dolphin. He also thinks he must be practical and try to eat all the fish now, before it rots in the sun. He wishes he could also feed the marlin, because it is his brother, but he realizes he must keep strong to kill the fish. After he finishes the tuna, Santiago takes the line in his right hand and calls upon God to help the cramp go away. He considers that if the cramp doesn't go away he may have to open the left hand forcibly if he needs it, which he is willing to do. For now, he decides to hope it will open on its own, since he knows he abused the hand in the night.

Santiago sees clouds building up and a flight of wild ducks and thinks that at sea no man is every truly alone. He knows that some fear being out of sight of land and are right to feel that way in months of sudden bad weather. Although this month is one of the hurricane months, he knows the weather is best at this time of year when there is no hurricane, and he sees no signs of one. He thinks about how a hurricane can be seen coming for days at sea, whereas ashore people do not see it coming because they don't know what to look for or perhaps the land makes a difference in the shape of the clouds. He considers the light breeze better for him than for the fish.

Santiago regards the cramp in his hand as a betrayal of his own body and a humiliation, and he wishes the boy were there to rub it for him. Suddenly, the fish makes its first jump, coming completely out of the water. The fish is beautiful and huge, two feet longer than the skiff. Its sword seems to Santiago like a baseball bat and tapered like a rapier; its tail seems like a scythe-blade. Santiago knows that he must keep pressure on the line so the fish doesn't run it out and that he must never let the fish learn its own strength. Santiago thinks that if he were the fish, he would pour everything into a run until something broke; but he thanks God that fish aren't as intelligent as those who kill them, though the fish are "more noble and more able."

Although in his lifetime, Santiago twice caught fish weighing a thousand pounds, he never did so alone and out of sight of land. He realizes he is now "fast to the biggest fish that he had ever seen and bigger than he had ever heard of" and that his hand surely will uncramp because his two hands and the fish and are brothers. Santiago wonders if the fish jumped to show itself to him. He wishes he could show himself to the fish but then decides that if the fish thinks Santiago is more man than he is, he will be so. Santiago momentarily wishes he were the fish, which has so much going for it against his intelligence and will. Although he is not religious, Santiago promises to say ten Our Fathers and ten Hail Marys and to make a pilgrimage to the Virgin of Cobre if he catches the marlin. He begins saying his prayers quickly and automatically. Afterwards, he feels better but is suffering just as much.

Santiago decides to rebait the other line in case he needs something more to eat. He's also running out of water. He doesn't think he'll be able to catch anything but a dolphin, though he wishes for a flying fish, which is excellent raw. Santiago thinks that he will kill this great fish, even though doing so is unjust, and show it "what a man can do and what a man endures." He also reminds himself that he told Manolin he was a strange old man and so now must prove it, though he has proven it a thousand times before.

Santiago decides to rest. He wishes that he could sleep and dream about the lions and then wonders why the lions are the main thing that is left to him. The marlin begins to swim at a higher level and turns a bit to the east, which Santiago previously thought of as signs that the fish is tiring and the current is pushing it more eastward. Santiago can picture the fish swimming below the water and wonders what it can see at that depth. And he remembers that he, like a cat, once saw well in the dark, though not absolute dark.

Santiago's hand finally uncramps, he shifts the line on his back, and thinks that he is tired and that if the fish is not tired, it is a very strange fish. He tries to think of baseball, of the New York Yankees and the Detroit Tigers and how this is the second day that he hasn't known what's happening. He tells himself he must have confidence and be worthy of the great DiMaggio, "who does all things perfectly even with the pain of the bone spur in his heel." He wonders momentarily what a bone spur really is.

Santiago thinks that "Man is not much beside the great birds and beasts" and that he'd rather be the marlin, unless the sharks come. He says, "If the sharks come, God pity him and me." Then Santiago considers that DiMaggio, whose father was a fisherman, would probably stay with a fish as long as Santiago has, unless the bone spur hurt too much.

As the sun sets, Santiago deliberately tries to give himself confidence by remembering in great detail the time in Casablanca when he arm wrestled for an entire day with "the great Negro from Cienfuegos who was the strongest man on the docks." Back then, Santiago was called *El Campeón* (the champion). By Monday, many bettors wanted the match called a draw, so they could go to work loading sacks of sugar or mining at the Havana Coal Company. But Santiago finished off his opponent before anyone had to go to work. For a long time afterward, everyone called him The Champion. The next year, few bets were placed on the return match, and Santiago easily beat the man, having already broken his spirit. Santiago won a few more matches, felt he could beat anyone, and then decided to give up arm wrestling because it might harm his right hand for fishing. He had tried his left, but "his left hand had always been a traitor and would not do what he called on it to do and he did not trust it."

Santiago sees a plane to Miami pass overhead and wonders what it would be like to fly low over the sea. He recalls the days when he used to watch the fish below from his seat in the mast-head of the turtle boats. As the sun goes down, he passes an island of Sargasso weed that heaves and sways as if the ocean were making love under a yellow blanket. Then Santiago catches a dolphin. Careful not to lose his hold on the line with the marlin, he brings in the dolphin, clubs it, and then rebaits the line and tosses it overboard.

Santiago notices that the marlin has slowed its pull on the line. He considers lashing the oars together across the stern to increase the boat's drag. He leans forward, pressing against the wood of the skiff so that it takes much of the strain of the line from his back. He feels good that he is learning the best way to handle the line and that he has eaten once and will again soon, while the great marlin has eaten nothing.

As the stars come out, Santiago thinks of them as his distant friends. He considers the marlin his friend, too, and marvels that he has never seen or heard of such a fish as this one, yet he must kill it. He considers that humans are lucky that they don't have to try to kill the stars, the sun, or the moon; it is bad enough they have to kill their brother creatures. Even as he remains determined to kill the marlin, Santiago feels sorry that it has had nothing to eat. He feels that the people it will feed are not worthy of this great fish.

Santiago decides to be cautious and not use the oars for drag, relying instead on the fish's hunger and its inability to understand what it is up against. He chooses instead to rest for a while, as much as he can, until his next duty. He determines to sleep to keep himself clear-headed, just as the stars, the moon, the sun, and even the ocean sleep. But he decides first to eat the dolphin.

When he guts the dolphin, he discovers two fresh flying fish inside. He positions himself in the boat, and when he washes the dolphin remains from his hands, he leaves a phosphorescent trail in the ocean. He also notices that the marlin's speed has slowed a bit. He eats half of one of the two dolphin fillets and one of the flying fish, thinking how miserable raw dolphin tastes. He wishes he had brought along salt and limes or had the foresight to splash water on the boat's bow, to evaporate and leave sea salt. He notices the clouds and says that there will be bad weather, but not for three or four days.

Santiago positions himself to sleep, pressing his body against his hand and rigging the line so that he cannot lose it in his sleep. He dreams at first of a school of porpoises during their mating time, jumping and diving back into the same hole. Then he dreams that he is asleep in his bed, cold from a north wind, and that his hand is asleep from his lying on it. Finally, he dreams of watching the lions from where the ship is anchored, and he is happy.

Santiago is jerked suddenly awake by the line racing out, and then the fish jumps several times. His hand and back are cut and burned, but he works very hard to make the marlin pay for every inch it drags out. Santiago wishes the boy were there to wet the lines and to be with him. Santiago wonders whether hunger or fear made the fish jump, though the fish seemed fearless, and then reminds himself that he must be fearless.

As the sun rises on his third day at sea, Santiago drags his cut right hand in the salt water to clean the cuts, and then he switches the line to his right and does the same for his left hand. He begins to think that the weakness in his left hand is because he didn't train it properly and that if it cramps again, the line can cut it off. But then he decides that thinking such a thing is evidence that he's beginning not to think clearly, so he eats the second flying fish. He thinks that he has done everything he can and that he's ready for the marlin to circle and the fight to come. Soon, he feels the marlin begin to turn.

Santiago continues to battle the marlin, pulling in line to shorten the fish's circles. Wet with sweat and aching, he sees black spots before his eyes but attributes them to the tension he is putting on the line.

Twice, he has felt weak and dizzy. He does not want to fail himself and die on a fish this great. So he asks God to help him endure and promises to say a hundred Our Fathers and a hundred Hail Marys. Because he cannot say the prayers now, he asks God to consider them said, promising to say them later. He feels the fish bang the leader with its sword. When Santiago feels the trade wind pick up, he begins to think hopefully that he'll need the wind to take the fish in. He thinks that he simply must steer south and west to head back, that a man never really gets lost at sea, and that Cuba is a long island.

On the fish's third circle, Santiago sees the fish pass under the boat. He can't believe the fish is so big. Eventually he sees the huge scythe blade of the fish's tail. Santiago prepared his harpoon long before, so now he reminds himself to be calm and strong and bring the fish in close. Many times, Santiago hauls the fish closer but the fish manages to right itself and swim away. Santiago thinks that the fish is killing him but that it has a right to, for he has never seen anything greater, more beautiful, calmer, or more noble than this fish he calls brother. He thinks, "Come on and kill me. I do not care who kills who." But he immediately tells himself to be clear headed and not think such things and to suffer like a man—or a fish. Against the fish's agony, Santiago pits all his pain, his remaining strength, and his long gone pride. Eventually he brings the fish close enough and, with all his strength, drives the harpoon in.

After killing the marlin that he calls brother, Santiago tells himself he must now do the slave work of lashing the fish to the boat and bringing it in. Santiago thinks of the fish as his fortune, although that is not why he wishes to touch the fish. He thinks about how he felt the marlin's heart when he drove in the harpoon. He also thinks about how he and the boy will splice the fishing lines that he now uses to fasten the marlin to the skiff. Although he thinks of the money the fish will bring, Santiago thinks even more of the fact that the great DiMaggio would be proud of him this day.

Santiago needs nourishment and moisture for the strength to bring the fish in, so he shakes some small shrimp out of a bed of seaweed, eats them, and drinks half of one of the two remaining drinks he has left in the water bottle. As he steers toward home, his head becomes a bit unclear, and he begins to wonder whether he is bringing the fish in or the fish is bringing him in. He thinks that he should let the fish bring him in, if doing so pleases the fish, for he has only bested the fish through trickery and the fish meant him no harm. As they speed together toward home, the old man keeps looking at the fish, to remind himself what he truly has done.

Within an hour, the first shark attacks. The attack is no accident. Following the scent of blood, the mako charges out of the depths, homing in. The mako is fast and fearless, well-armed, built to feed on all the fish in the sea, and beautiful except for its jaws. Most of all, it is no scavenger. Its teeth are long, like an old man's fingers, but crisped like claws. Santiago prepares the harpoon, though the rope is short because of what he cut away to lash the marlin to the skiff. His head is clear now and he realizes how little he can do to prevent the shark from hitting the marlin. Still, he hopes to get the shark, and he wishes bad luck to its mother.

The mako tears into the marlin just above the tail. Santiago, who knows where the shark's brain is located, drives the harpoon in with all his strength, resolution, and hatred. After the shark dies, Santiago assesses that the shark took about 40 pounds of the marlin, his harpoon, and all his rope. As the marlin bleeds anew, Santiago cannot bear to look at the mutilated fish. He knows more sharks will come, drawn by the blood. For a moment, he tries to console himself that he killed the mako, the biggest he has ever seen. He wishes he was at home in bed and only dreaming that he caught the marlin. But then he quickly reminds himself, "A man can be destroyed but not defeated."

As bad as he feels, Santiago must sail on and take what is coming. Still, he knows that he can't stop thinking; that and baseball are all he has left. So he wonders if the great DiMaggio would have liked the way he stabbed the mako in the brain. He wonders if his own injured hands were as great a handicap in his battle with the shark as DiMaggio's bone spurs, though he doesn't know what bone spurs are. He also tries to cheer himself by affirming that every moment he is drawing nearer to home and that the skiff sails lighter for the loss of the forty pounds.

Santiago knows more sharks will come. At first, he can think of nothing he can do against them. Then suddenly he realizes that he can lash his knife to one of the oars. That way, though he is an old man, he won't be unarmed. He considers it silly, even a sin not to have hope. For a moment, he claims not to want to think about sin because he doesn't understand it and doesn't believe in it. Yet he wonders if it was a sin to kill the fish, even though he did so to keep himself alive and to feed many people. He also recognizes that he killed the fish out of pride and because he was born to be a fisherman—like San Pedro (St. Peter) and the great DiMaggio's father—just as the fish was born to be a fish. He wonders whether killing the marlin was not a sin because he loved it—or whether that made killing it even more of a sin. He admits that he enjoyed killing the mako shark, which lives on live fish as he does and is not a scavenger, but beautiful, noble, and fearless. Eventually, Santiago decides that he killed the shark in self-defense and killed it well, that all animals kill one another, and that fishing kills him even as it keeps him alive. Then he reminds himself that the boy keeps him alive and that he mustn't deceive himself too much.

Santiago pulls off a piece of the marlin's meat, where the shark cut it. He tastes it, noticing the quality and noting that it would bring the highest price in the market. Yet he cannot keep the scent out of the water, so he knows more sharks will come. For two hours he sails, occasionally resting and chewing a bit more of the marlin to be strong. When he sees the first of the two shovel-nosed sharks, he says, "Ay," an involuntary noise that a man might make "feeling the nail go through his hands and into the wood."

The two shovel-nosed sharks—Santiago calls them *galanos*—are stupid from hunger but closing in on the marlin. These sharks are different from the mako. They are bad smelling and scavengers as well as killers. They are the kind that cut off a sleeping turtle's legs and flippers or hit a man in the water, if they're hungry, even though the man has no blood or fish scent on him.   They even hit the marlin differently, shaking the skiff as they jerk and pull at the meat.

With his injured hands, Santiago raises the oar with the knife lashed to it and drives it into the brain of one of the sharks and into its eye, killing it. Santiago swings the boat to reveal the second shark and stabs it, barely piercing its hide but hurting his own hands and shoulder. Then he repeatedly stabs it in the head, the eye, and the brain until it is dead.

After he cleans the blade and gets back on course, Santiago thinks that the two shovel-nosed sharks must have taken a quarter of the marlin, and he apologizes to the great fish. He tells it, "I shouldn't have gone out so far, fish." Then he adds, "Neither for you or for me." He checks the lashing on the knife and wishes he had a stone to sharpen it. He admonishes himself not to wish for what he didn't bring with him but to focus on what he can still do to defend the marlin. He says aloud that he gives himself much good advice but that he is tired of it. He tries to remember that the skiff is much lighter now and not think of the marlin's mutilation. He thinks that the great fish would have kept a man all winter but then tries not to think of that either. He wishes catching the marlin had been a dream but then thinks that it might have turned out well.

When the next shovel-nosed shark comes like a pig to a trough, Santiago stabs it and kills it, but the knife blade snaps. He doesn't even watch the dead shark falling away into the deep water, growing smaller and smaller, although that always fascinates him. Instead, he feels beaten. He feels too old to club sharks yet decides he will try with the oars, the club, and any other items left in the boat. He admits that he is more than tired now; he is tired inside.

At sunset, the sharks hit again. Santiago knows he must let the sharks get a good hold on the marlin and then club them. He does so with the first shark, hitting it on the head and then the nose, until it slides away from the marlin. The second shark has been feeding on the marlin and already has pieces of meat in its jaws. When Santiago clubs it, it only looks at him and wrenches away more meat. When the shark comes again, Santiago hits it repeatedly until it slides away. For a while he doesn't see them, but then he sees one swimming in circles. He knows he couldn't expect to kill them, though he could have in his time, but he has hurt them both badly and would have killed the first one if he had used a bat.

He tries not to think about the marlin, which is half ruined now. As night falls, he knows he will soon see the glow of Havana or one of the new beaches, and he hopes no one has been worried. He thinks at first that there is only Manolin to worry, though he knows the young man would have confidence in him. But then he realizes that some of the older fishermen will worry and some others, too; and he thinks, "I live in a good town."

Santiago apologizes again to the marlin for going so far out. He tells the fish that together he and it have ruined many sharks and wonders how many sharks the marlin killed in its lifetime with its spear. He believes that if he'd had a hatchet he could have lashed the marlin's bill to an oar and fought with that, which would have made a formidable weapon. He wonders what he will do now when the sharks come in the night but remains determined to fight them, even until he is dead.

Santiago knows from his pain that he is not dead. He remembers all the prayers he promised to say if he caught the fish but is too tired to say them now. He hopes for some luck to bring in the half of the fish he has left and wonders whether he violated his luck by going out too far. Then he decides that he is being silly and needs to concentrate. He wishes he could buy some luck and wonders whether he might buy it with his broken knife, lost harpoon, and two bad hands. He thinks that might be possible, since he nearly bought some luck with his 84 days at sea without a catch. Then he thinks that he would take some luck in any form and pay whatever price was asked and that right now he wishes to see the glow of Havana's light.

Around 10 o'clock, he does see the glow. He is stiff and sore and hopes not to fight again. But around midnight, the sharks come in a pack. He can barely see them, although he feels them shaking the skiff as they tear at the marlin. He clubs desperately at what he can only feel in the dark, until something seizes the club. He continues to beat at them with the tiller, until the tiller smashes. Then he lunges at a shark with the splintered butt, driving in the sharp end until the shark rolls away. After that, no more sharks come, for there is nothing left of the marlin to eat.

Injured, Santiago can hardly breathe and has a coppery sweet taste in his mouth. Defiantly, he spits into the ocean, telling the sharks to eat his spit and dream they've killed a man. He knows he's utterly beaten. He fits the damaged tiller into the rudder and continues toward home, trying not to think or feel and ignoring the sharks that occasionally come to pick at the remaining bits of marlin. He notices only how light and fast the skiff is and that the boat is not really harmed except for the tiller, which can be repaired. Following the lights in toward shore, he thinks that the wind can sometimes be a friend, that the sea contains both friends and enemies, that his own bed can be a friend, and that to be beaten is very easy. When he asks himself what really beat him, he answers honestly that nothing beat him; he just went out too far. Long after midnight, when everyone else is asleep, he finally comes ashore.

Commentary

This second section of the part that takes place at sea is much longer than either of the two parts that take place on land and comprises the story's central action and its most dramatic moments. While Santiago's struggles in this section can be viewed collectively (as some critics have suggested) as a single trial lasting three days, they can also be considered according to his three principal adversaries: the marlin, the mako shark, and the shovel-nosed sharks. Either way, each challenge is at once game and rite, requiring both luck and faith.

In this section, Hemingway increasingly shifts from the omniscient narrator to Santiago's perspective, combining narrative modes with devices such as letting Santiago talk aloud to himself, presenting a third-person narration of his thoughts, and drifting subtly from either of these into a kind of interior monologue. To convey this limited *stream of consciousness* (a depiction of the actual flow of thoughts and feelings as they pass through a character's mind), Hemingway simulates a supposed disorganization in the way thoughts leap into the old man's fatigued mind. Yet the technique actually relies on a loose connection of ideas deliberately tied together through recurring images, allusions, actions, and themes.

Throughout this section, Hemingway fully dramatizes actions and themes that he introduced or foreshadowed in the novella's previous pages. For example, several incidents appropriate to this marine setting anticipate the section's significant battles: the man-of-war bird chasing the flying fish suggests Santiago trying to land the great winged marlin; the tired warbler harried by hawks anticipates the worn out Santiago's struggle with the sharks. Here, Hemingway also reintroduces the earlier baseball allusions and images, and the themes those allusions and images advance. When the marlin first jumps, Santiago describes its sword as the length of a baseball bat. After his battle with the shovel-nosed sharks, Santiago wishes he had had a bat. In both cases, Hemingway again connects the marlin and Santiago to the endurance and nobility of the great DiMaggio. Hemingway also unfolds and further dramatizes Santiago's prodigious skill as a fisherman and his dedication to his craft. And Hemingway again yokes a belief in luck with religious conviction, as when Santiago alternates between wishing for luck in catching the fish (which he is afraid to mention for fear it won't happen) and praying to God to make the great fish swallow the bait, to help him land the fish, and to help him defend the fish against the sharks.

Supporting this reintroduction or repetition of actions, images, allusions, and themes, Hemingway uses a stylistic technique of repeating sounds and rhythms, words and sentence structures. For example, when Santiago prepares to eat the dolphin fillets and the two flying fish he found inside the dolphin, Hemingway writes, "Back in the bow he laid the two fillets of fish out on the wood with the flying fish beside them." The use of language (in this case, the repetition of sounds)

suggests incantation and ritual and serves the same function as the catechism-like structure of earlier conversations with Manolin, thereby reinforcing the same images, allusions, and themes.

These repetitions and reintroductions complement the novella's many cycles: For example, the novella's basic structure comes from Santiago's journey from the land, to the sea, and back to the land again. The nature of all life consists of a passing on of collective knowledge and memory from one generation to the next, as well as a passage from youth to old age. The natural order binds together all creatures in mutual dependency and a common fate as hunter and hunted, predator and prey. (As Santiago points out, "everything kills everything else" in the world.) Even Santiago's fate represents a cycle—from the failure of 84 days without a catch, to the hard-won victory over the marlin, to the tragedy of its loss to the sharks, to the redemption at the story's end.

Character Insight

From the moment Santiago feels the marlin's first tug at the other end of the line, he feels connected to it in a variety of ways, as he does to his brothers the flying fish, the turtles, and the porpoises. Oftentimes, Santiago *anthropomorphizes* (endows with human characteristics and feelings) the creatures he feels connected to. So he refers to the marlin as "he," although he cannot know its gender. As he and the great fish remain locked in battle, he first pities and admires the fish and then empathizes and identifies with it. When the marlin lurches forward and the line cuts Santiago's hand, he immediately assumes that something must have hurt the marlin, as he himself is hurt. He muses that both he and the fish have made choices that inevitably led them to be locked in this life-and-death struggle, isolated, with no one to help either of them. Just as the marlin was born to be a fish, Santiago reflects, he was born to be a fisherman. In the inevitability of their circumstances and their suffering, both seem reminiscent of Job.

Santiago also resembles St. Francis of Assisi in recognizing the connection of all living creatures. His conversation with the warbler bird that must eventually face the hawks as it heads toward land is just one example. When Santiago's own left hand cramps, he feels betrayed and humiliated by it, and his attitude and response suggest St. Francis of Assisi's mockery of his body as "Brother Ass" whenever it failed him in his calling. In fact, recurring references to the cramped left hand (and the old man's claws) compare it to the eagle's claws, the hawk's claws, even the shark's teeth that are crisped like claws.

So while Hemingway the journalist presents the story's creatures in accurate detail, he also frequently uses them to suggest the thoughts, emotions, or circumstances of his characters. Hemingway uses the marlin to represent not only a great fish locked in an evenly balanced and protracted battle with an accomplished fisherman (much like Santiago's lengthy arm-wrestling contest with the Negro from Cienfuegos) but a creature possessing the same qualities that Santiago possesses, admires, and hopes to pass on to the boy: nobility of spirit, greatness in living, faithfulness to one's own identity and ways, endurance, beauty, and dignity.

Although Santiago momentarily contemplates the price the great fish may bring in the market, what he really wonders is whether the fish has plans or is simply desperate as he is. What Santiago desperately wants is one epic catch—not just to survive, but to prove once more his skill, reassert his identity as a fisherman, secure his reputation in the community, and ensure for all time that Manolin will indeed become his successor in what matters most in life. Here, Santiago (and by extension Hemingway) considers whether some design exists in the natural world and its endless cycles that can somehow redeem the individual life from meaningless.

The fundamental message in Santiago's connection to all the creatures linked to him—the flying fish, turtle, marlin, warbler, mako shark—is that noble as he and they are, they all remain subject to nature and so must eventually face destruction in the immutable natural order where "everything kills everything else" and also nourishes everything else. As critics such as Katharine Jobes have pointed out, this is part of the conservation of life, the physical law that says no energy is ever lost but simply transformed in a physical (and here spiritual) assimilation. What redeems the individual life from meaningless in nature's endless cycle is to use one's skills, and what nature has bestowed, to live with great fervor and then to accept destruction with dignity, passing on whatever one can to a successor. So Santiago determines to show "what a man can do and what a man endures" and to prove that he is indeed "a strange old man." In this way, he truly can be "destroyed but not defeated."

As Santiago and the marlin struggle, Santiago repeatedly wishes he had the boy to help him and to see this great battle. When Santiago simultaneously wishes for the boy and for some salt to make palatable the raw tuna he must eat to sustain his strength, he yokes his need for the boy's love and respect (to sustain his soul) with his need to eat the raw tuna (to sustain his body). Each time Santiago wishes for "the boy" in a moment of crisis, he invokes the strength and courage of his own youth, as well as the presence of Manolin (as critics such as Carlos Baker have suggested). Each time, Santiago relies upon his "trick" of imaginative vision to draw into himself the youthful vigor and inspiration he needs to sustain himself. In this way, his thoughts of "the boy" keep him strong and resolute as he faces each new hardship.

Santiago again relies on this "trick" when he gives himself confidence to "stay with the fish" by thinking of the great DiMaggio, who endured the pain of a bone spur to make a great comeback and whose father was a great fisherman. Santiago hopes to be "worthy of the great DiMaggio who does all things perfectly" and later believes that DiMaggio would be proud of him for staying with the fish despite his suffering. Santiago also uses this "trick" when he recalls in great detail his protracted contest with the Negro from Cienfuegos, the contest in which Santiago first earned the title of The Champion (*El Campeón*).

So Santiago assumes vital strength and spiritual nourishment from his own youthful self, from Manolin, from DiMaggio, and from the Negro from Cienfuegos. That also explains why, when Santiago dreams, the lions are all that he has left. The lions, too, are a source of inspiration. The lions (like "the boy") are identified with both Santiago's youthful self and Manolin and with such qualities as greatness, nobility, vitality, strength, and even immortality. So the lions are what is left because Santiago's imaginative vision is what he has left to rely upon.

Eventually, Santiago kills the great marlin and lashes it alongside the skiff so that the beautiful creature he admires, identifies with, and calls brother seems to be bringing him in rather than he bringing it in. Santiago says he is only better than the fish through "trickery," meaning both the tricks of his trade and that capacity for imaginative vision that he uses to keep strong and resolute. Interestingly, that same imaginative vision demands something to redeem the individual life as the price for acceptance of life's natural cycles.

The death of the marlin represents Santiago's greatest victory and the promise of all those intangibles he so desperately hopes for, to redeem his individual life. Yet Hemingway reports almost matter-of-factly that Santiago enjoys this victory for only an hour before the first shark comes. The omniscient narrator tells us, "The shark was not an accident." Inevitably, as victor, Santiago must fall subject to nature's endless cycle and life's tragedy. Like the marlin, Santiago must lose and become victim. The mako is the largest, strongest, fiercest shark Santiago has ever seen—yet beautiful, noble, and fearless. Consequently, the mako also is identified with Santiago as it assumes its rightful place in the natural order. As hunter (not scavenger), it obeys nature's ordinances and remains true to its own ways.

After Santiago drives in the harpoon and kills the mako, he knows more sharks will come. The mako has ripped away about 40 pounds of the marlin's meat, and a great cloud of blood trails behind in the water. (Again, biblical significances resonate in the number 40 and in the mixing of water and blood.) To keep himself strong, Santiago eats a piece of the marlin, whom he has said no one is "worthy of eating." Several critics have seen this act as a kind of communion. As Santiago partakes of the great fish, he becomes one with it. As a result, the marlin's death is not meaningless, for the fish fortifies the old man, providing him both physical and spiritual nourishment. Santiago also seems to gain the ability to accept and rise above his suffering, his defeat, and the inevitability of death. In so doing, he gains the capacity to endure, perform the best he can, and go down with dignity.

Somehow this newfound acceptance also affects Santiago's relationship with the people of his village. Whereas before he went far out from the land (and its "traps and treacheries") to the deepest parts of the ocean where the deepest thoughts also can be plumbed, he now seems closer to the community he left behind:

> I hope no one has been too worried. There is only the boy to worry, of course. But I am sure he would have confidence. Many of the older fishermen will worry. Many others too, he thought. I live in a good town.

After partaking of the marlin, Santiago is associated with symbols of the crucifixion that were associated with the marlin until its death, as critics such as Philip Young and Arvin Wells have noted. (Later, other allusions to Christ will be associated with Manolin.) For example, the omniscient narrator describes the sound Santiago makes when he sees the shovel-nosed sharks as "just a noise such as a man might make, involuntarily, feeling the nail go through his hands and into the wood." But the image (a rare instance in which the writing seems a bit heavy-handed) is used in a decidedly non-Christian manner to represent suffering, seeming defeat, and the endurance through which one redeems an individual life within nature's tragic cycle. Immediately afterward, the marlin's brave and unavailing struggle to save its own life becomes Santiago's brave and unavailing struggle to save the marlin from the sharks.

Theme

In killing the mako, Santiago loses his harpoon—the first of many such losses as he continues a futile battle with the shovel-nosed sharks. One-by-one, Santiago looses what few tools he has left in the boat, yet he vows to go on fighting until he has nothing left or is dead. Unlike the mako, the shovel-nosed sharks are scavengers. Their desecration of the marlin suggests Santiago's derision by the younger, mechanized fishermen who embrace the new materialism as progress. As the scavenger sharks rob Santiago of his victory, the pragmatic younger fishermen rob the natural world and the dedicated fishermen of intrinsic, less tangible values and spiritually satisfying meaning. Even so, the scavenger sharks and the mechanized fishermen inevitably must win— at least for a time.

Suggesting the marlin's wound from the harpoon and the crucified Christ's wound from the soldier's lance, something in Santiago's chest ruptures during his last battle with a shovel-nosed shark. He has trouble breathing and tastes the sweet, coppery taste of his own blood. (Whether or not Santiago will die shortly after his return to land, he will never know another heroic moment at sea or tie into another epic catch.) Thoroughly beaten, Santiago no longer fights the scavenger sharks that briefly come up to nibble away the last bits from the marlin's skeletal remains. The fish has been stripped of all material value, and Santiago apologizes to the fish for going so far out to sea and ruining them both.

Ever since the mako's first attack, Santiago has wondered whether killing the marlin was a great sin. He eventually decides that he has no answer for that. He only knows that he killed the marlin not just to sell for food but for pride and because he is a fisherman like St. Peter (*San Pedro*) and the great DiMaggio's father. In this understanding resides an echo of God's answer to Job when he asked why the good are made to suffer. Essentially, God's reply is that suffering is in the very nature of the universe. Just as enigmatic, Santiago's understanding is that he did what he had to do, what he was born to do, and what his role in the eternal nature of things demanded. As he sails on in, following the lights on the beach, Santiago wonders what it was that actually beat him. Answering honestly, he admits that nothing actually beat him— he simply went out too far.

Glossary

brisa (Spanish) breeze.

calambre (Spanish) cramp (muscular).

rapier a slender, two-edged sword with a large, cupped hilt.

scythe a tool with a long, single-edged blade set at an angle on a long, curved handle, used in cutting long grass, grain, and so on, by hand.

Gran Ligas (Spanish) the two main leagues of professional baseball clubs in the U.S., the National League and the American League: also the Major Leagues.

Tigres (Spanish) reference to the Detroit Tigers.

juegos (Spanish) games.

un espuela de hueso a bone spur.

Casablanca seaport in northwest Morocco, on the Atlantic.

Cienfuegos seaport on the south coast of Cuba.

El Campeón (Spanish) The Champion.

masthead the top part of a ship's mast.

dorado (Spanish) gilding or gilt (literally); here a descriptive term for the golden dolphin.

Rigel a supergiant, multiple star, usually the brightest star in the constellation Orion.

dentuso (Spanish) big-toothed; (in Cuba) a particularly voracious and frightening species of shark with rows of large, sharp teeth; here, a descriptive term for the mako shark.

shovel-nosed having a broad, flattened nose, head, or bill.

galanos (Spanish) mottled ones (literally); here a descriptive term for the shovel-nosed sharks.

Part Four
Back Ashore

Summary

When Santiago reaches shore, everyone is in bed, so no one is there to help him. He pulls the skiff up onto the beach as best he can, makes the boat fast to a rock, and then carries the furled mast on his shoulder toward his shack. Looking back, he sees in the reflection from the street light the marlin's great tail standing up way behind the skiff.

As he starts to climb, Santiago falls. He tries to get up but can't, so he sits there, with the mast on his shoulder. He watches a cat going about its business. Eventually he gets up again. Five times he falls and has to sit down again before he finally reaches his shack. Finally inside, he leans the mast against a wall and finds the water bottle in the dark and takes a drink. He lies down on the cot, pulls the blanket over himself, and sleeps face down on the newspapers, with his arms straight out and palms up.

Santiago is still asleep the next morning when Manolin comes to the shack to check on him as the young man has done every morning since Santiago put to sea. Manolin has slept late this morning because a strong, blowing wind is keeping the drifting boats from going out. Manolin cries when he sees the old man's injured hands and quietly goes out to get the old man some coffee.

Outside, many fishermen are gathered around the skiff, and one of them is measuring the marlin's remains. The fishermen ask Manolin how Santiago is, and Manolin tells them that Santiago is sleeping and not to disturb him. When the fisherman who is measuring the great fish reports that it is 18 feet long, Manolin replies, "I believe it."

From Martin, the proprietor at the Terrace, Manolin gets coffee with plenty of milk and sugar. Martin says, "What a fish . . . . There has never been such a fish." Then he also praises Manolin's two fish, but the boy isn't interested. He tells Martin that he'll be back when he knows what Santiago can eat and that in the meantime, no one should disturb the old man. Martin replies, "Tell him how sorry I am."

Santiago sleeps so long and hard that Manolin has to go across the road to borrow wood to reheat the coffee. Eventually the old man does awaken, and after he drinks some of the coffee, he tells Manolin, "They beat me." Manolin responds adamantly that the great fish didn't beat him, and Santiago explains it was after he caught the fish that he was defeated.

Manolin tells Santiago that Pedrico is taking care of the skiff and the gear and wants to know what Santiago wants done with the fish. Santiago tells Manolin to give Pedrico the head to chop up and use in fish traps and then offers Manolin the spear. Manolin replies that he wants the fish's spear. When Santiago asks whether anyone searched for him, Manolin tells him they did, with coast guard and planes. Santiago replies that the ocean is very large and the skiff small. He notices how welcome it is to have someone to talk to after three days of talking to himself.

When Santiago asks about Manolin's catch, Manolin tells the old man that he caught four fish, but now he will fish with Santiago again. Santiago says no, because he is not lucky. But Manolin says to hell with luck; he'll bring the luck with him. Santiago asks what the young man's family will say, and Manolin replies that he doesn't care and still has much to learn from Santiago.

Thinking about the past three days, Santiago tells Manolin that they must have a killing lance, that they can make the blade out of spring leaf from an old Ford, and that they can get it in Guanabacoa and have it ground to make it sharp. He also mentions that his knife broke. Manolin says he'll get Santiago another knife and then asks the old man how many days of *brisa* (breeze) are left. When Santiago tells him three days, the young man says he'll get everything ready, and Santiago only needs to get his hands well. Santiago replies that he knows how to care for the hands but that something broke in his chest. The boy tells him to get his chest well, too.

Manolin says he's going out to get the old man a clean shirt and some food, and Santiago asks for the newspapers for the time he was gone. Manolin again tells the old man to get well, for there is much the old man can teach him, and then asks how much the old man suffered. Santiago replies that he suffered plenty. Manolin says he'll also get the old man some medicine for his hands, and Santiago reminds him to give the marlin's head to Pedrico. As Manolin walks down the road, he cries again.

That afternoon, some tourists at the Terrace see the remains of the marlin—now just so much garbage waiting to go out with the tide—and they ask a waiter what it is. The waiter, trying to explain to the couple what happened to the marlin, says *tiburon* (shark). Misunderstanding, the tourists remark to one another that they didn't know sharks had such beautiful tails. Back in his shack, with the boy sitting beside him, Santiago sleeps again and dreams of the lions.

Commentary

Literary
Device

This third, brief part of the novella completes the cycle of Santiago's journey from the land to the sea and back to the land again. The narrative returns to the third-person, omniscient narration of the first part (which also takes places on land), pulling back from previous explorations of Santiago's thoughts. For example, the narrative simply reports that Santiago knows "the depth of his tiredness" and objectively describes what Santiago sees when he looks back at the marlin's skeleton beside the beached skiff, without moving into his thoughts. Just as the earlier transition into his thoughts when he is alone at sea is intuitive and logical, the depth of Santiago's exhaustion helps smooth this shift back to the earlier narrative mode.

The story benefits from this controlled reporting and psychic distance because all the earlier preparations and foreshadowing assure that the emotional impact of Santiago's tragedy is not lost on readers, but instead resonates within them without *melodrama* (that is, without unearned sensationalism and extravagant emotional appeal). Santiago has been wholly beaten by the scavenger sharks—those swimming appetites and natural scavengers that Hemingway equates with the pragmatic fishermen and the new materialism, as well as with the inevitable destruction inherent in nature's order and the natural cycle of life. The marlin has been picked clean of all practical and material value, and its earlier association with the crucified Christ (a non-Christian representation of suffering, defeat, and the endurance through which one redeems an individual life within nature's tragic cycle) has been fully conveyed to Santiago.

Character
Insight

Although his name is Spanish for St. James (a fisherman and disciple), Santiago arrives while Manolin and others who might help with the skiff and gear are sleeping, just as Christ kept watch at Gethsemane while the disciples slept. Santiago carries the mast up the hill toward home and looks back at the marlin's skeleton, as Christ carried the cross to Golgotha, "the place of a skull." Santiago sits down five times under the burden of the mast, as Christ fell under the burden of the cross. And when Santiago finally lies down in bed, he sleeps with his arms straight out, in the position of the crucified Christ.

Theme

Yet, like the biblical authors, Hemingway doesn't leave the story in unredeemed tragedy. As the mechanical fisherman and their practical materialism must eventually triumph, their inevitable undoing is also embedded in their methods and their philosophy. As all living creatures are both predator and prey in the natural order, all also nourish one another. As Christ must submit to the crucifixion, his resurrection also gives hope and the promise of eternal life. As Santiago must accept his role in the natural order and the cycle of human existence, his suffering, endurance, and nobility in defeat also redeem his individual life. And as Santiago's epic catch (stripped of all practical and material worth) must eventually wash out with the tide as so much garbage, the skeleton still manages to become a vehicle for the intrinsic values Santiago craves most to give his existence meaning and dignity.

The first evidence of this redemption comes the next morning. Manolin discovers Santiago and sees his wounded hands (wounds that suggest the stigmata). Crying, the young man goes to fetch the old man some coffee. Along the way, he sees a group of fishermen clustered around the marlin's remains, still lashed to the skiff. One of the fishermen is measuring the skeleton and reports with admiration that the marlin was 18 feet from nose to tail. Manolin, who has already seen the great skeleton, responds, "I believe it." When Manolin arrives at the Terrace, the proprietor Martin says, "What a fish . . . . There has never been such a fish." Clearly, the skeletal evidence of Santiago's epic catch is already becoming the stuff of legend, securing forever his reputation in the community.

Character Insight

Manolin's expression of faith in the marlin's epic size is just the beginning of his credo embracing the old man, his abilities, and the philosophy by which he lives his life. Manolin keeps watch as Santiago sleeps and even reheats the old man's coffee. When Santiago finally awakens and tells Manolin, "They beat me," Manolin is the one who interprets Santiago's great struggle. "*He* didn't beat you. Not the fish." In this second affirmation, Manolin lives up to the true significance of his name (which is short for Emmanuel), thereby conveying his own association with Christ the Redeemer, though again the association is used in a non-Christian manner. Manolin articulates for Santiago the true meaning of his great struggle. Santiago was not beaten by the fish but by the inevitability of nature's cycle. And though beaten, his great suffering and endurance nonetheless bring redemption. Manolin helps Santiago recognize that he has successfully reasserted his identity as an incomparable fisherman, proving once again his dedication to his craft and the value of the philosophy from which that dedication springs.

In accepting the marlin's spear, Manolin accepts for all time Santiago's legacy. The spear can variously suggest the cross, the sword of knighthood (so valued by Don Quixote), the flag of Santiago's way of life, a token from the natural world, or simply the only thing Santiago has left to offer as a symbol of all the intangibles he so desperately wishes to leave the young man. Regardless, Manolin accepts the spear with a clear understanding of its significance, taking a sort of oath that becomes his third expression of faith (which is once again yoked to luck). He tells Santiago, "Now we fish together again." And when Santiago offers the usual reasons against this course of action, Manolin replies, "The hell with luck . . . I'll bring the luck with me . . . I still have much to learn."

Style & Language

Santiago now clearly understands that he has ensured for all time that Manolin will become his successor in what matters most in life. He resumes their habitual way of conversing and shares something of his recent great struggle. "We must get a good killing lance," he tells Manolin, recalling his earlier need. In all their plans to fish together again, the reader hears the familiar cadences and formality of ritual and catechism. The reader also clearly hears the familiar fictions of the novella's first part (those fictions of a winning lottery ticket or a cast net that had already been sold). Working within the psychic distance of the third-person, omniscient narrative, Hemingway takes great care to avoid any definitive conclusion about whether the old man is dying from the "something" in his chest that is broken. Whether he dies immediately, or soon enough from age and circumstances, the story remains the same. Santiago has secured for himself the only individual redemption and immortality possible to human beings. That is why, when he later dreams, he dreams again of the lions that represent his own youth, the qualities he leaves Manolin, and his immortality.

In living according to his own code of behavior, accepting the natural order and cycle of life, struggling and enduring and redeeming his individual existence through his life's work, and passing on to the next generation everything of value that he has gained, Santiago becomes an *everyman* (an archetypal representation of the human condition). As such, his story becomes genuinely uplifting. Readers of different ages and levels of understanding can find something inspirational in the story, just as the tourists, who mistake the marlin for a shark, still comprehend from its skeleton something of the great fish's grandeur.

Glossary

spring leaf   curved plate that supports the vehicle above the suspension components and allows vertical suspension movement: also leaf spring; here the words are probaby presented in reverse order as they would be in Spanish.

Guanabacoa   one of the oldest European settlements in Cuba; now part of the urban conglomerate of present-day Havana.

barracuda   any of a family of fierce, pikelike tropical fish: some species are edible.

tiburon   (Spanish) shark.

CHARACTER ANALYSES

The following character analyses delve into the physical, emotional, and psychological traits of the literary work's major characters so that you might better understand what motivates these characters. The writer of this study guide provides this scholarship as an educational tool by which you may compare your own interpretations of the characters. Before reading the character analyses that follow, consider first writing your own short essays on the characters as an exercise by which you can test your understanding of the original literary work. Then, compare your essays to those that follow, noting discrepancies between the two. If your essays appear lacking, that might indicate that you need to re-read the original literary work or re-familiarize yourself with the major characters.

Santiago

Santiago is an impoverished old man who has endured many ordeals, whose best days are behind him, whose wife has died, and who never had children. For 84 days, he has gone without catching the fish upon which his meager existence, the community's respect, and his sense of identity as an accomplished fisherman all depend. As a result, the young man who is like a son to him (the young man who, since the age of five, has fished with him and learned from him) now fishes, at the behest of his parents, with another fisherman.

Indeed, Santiago's philosophy and internal code of behavior make him unconventional in his society (as critics such as Bickford Sylvester have mentioned). Santiago's dedication to his craft (beyond concerns of material gain or survival) separates him from the pragmatic fishermen motivated by money. He stands apart from Cuba's evolution to a new materialism and a village fishing culture converting to a fishing industry. He remains dedicated to a profession he sees as a more spiritual way of life and a part of nature's order in the eternal cycle that makes all creatures brothers in their common condition of both predator and prey.

What Santiago desperately wants is one epic catch—not just to survive, but to prove once more his skill, reassert his identity as a fisherman, secure his reputation in the community, and ensure for all time that Manolin will forever honor his memory and become his successor in what matters most in life. For Santiago, what matters most in life is to live with great fervor and nobility according to his beliefs, to use his skills and nature's gifts to the best of his ability, to struggle and endure and redeem his individual existence through his life's work, to accept inevitable destruction with dignity, and to pass on to the next generation everything of value that he has gained. In these desires, he reflects the desires of us all.

What makes Santiago special is that despite a lifetime of hardships that have hurt him (as the morning sun has always hurt his eyes), he is still a man in charge and an expert who knows the tricks of his fisherman's craft. His eyes remain young, cheerful, and undefeated. He knows how to rely on the transcendent power of his own imagination to engender the inspiration and confidence he needs and to keep alive in himself and others the hope, dreams, faith, absorption, and resolution to transcend hardship.

Manolin

Manolin is Santiago's last and deepest human relationship, his replacement in the generational cycle of human existence, the one to whom he wishes to entrust his skill as a fisherman, the transforming power of his vision, and his memory. As Santiago is mentor, spiritual father, and the old man or old age, Manolin is pupil, son, and the boy or youth. Manolin loves and cares for Santiago, and at the story's end, he professes his faith in Santiago and everything Santiago represents. Living up to his name, which is the diminutive of Manuel (Spanish for Emmanuel, the Redeemer), Manolin articulates for Santiago the true meaning of his great struggle, which has brought him the intangibles he craves. Three times, Manolin professes his faith in Santiago. In accepting the marlin's spear, Manolin demonstrates once and for all that he clearly understands and accepts all that Santiago wishes to bequeath him—and all that comes with that inheritance.

Marlin

The marlin is more than a great fish locked in an evenly balanced and protracted battle with an accomplished fisherman. It is also a creature onto whom Santiago projects the same qualities that he possesses, admires, and hopes to pass on: nobility of spirit, greatness in living, faithfulness to one's own identity and ways, endurance, beauty, and dignity. As Santiago and the marlin remain locked in battle for three days, they become intimately connected. Santiago first pities and admires the fish and then empathizes and identifies with it. He recognizes that just as the marlin was born to be a fish, he was born to be a fisherman. They are brothers in the inevitability of their circumstances, locked in the natural cycle of predator and prey.

The marlin's death represents Santiago's greatest victory and the promise of all those intangibles he so desperately hopes for to redeem his individual existence. Yet, like the marlin, Santiago also must inevitably lose and become the victim. After the mako shark's attack, Santiago eats the marlin's flesh to sustain himself, completing the natural cycle in which the great creature passes on something of itself to Santiago. Not only are all creatures predator and prey, but all also nourish one another. Allusions to the crucified Christ that were previously associated with the marlin (images that represent suffering, apparent defeat, and the endurance through which one redeems an individual life within nature's tragic cycle) are transferred to Santiago (as critics such as Philip Young and Arvin Wells have suggested). The marlin's brave and unavailing struggle to save its own life becomes Santiago's brave an unavailing struggle to save the marlin from the scavenger sharks.

The scavenger sharks strip the marlin of all material value, leaving only its skeleton lashed to Santiago's skiff. But before that skeleton ends up as so much garbage to be washed out with the tide, it becomes a mute testimony to Santiago's greatness and the vehicle for those intrinsic values Santiago craves to give his existence meaning and dignity. The fisherman who measures the marlin's skeleton reports that it is 18 feet long—evidence of the largest fish the villagers have ever known to come out of the Gulf. And when Manolin accepts the marlin's spear, he accepts for all time everything that Santiago wishes to bequeath him.

CRITICAL ESSAYS

On the pages that follow, the writer of this study guide provides critical scholarship on various aspects of Hemingway's *The Old Man and the Sea*. These interpretive essays are intended solely to enhance your understanding of the original literary work; they are supplemental materials and are not to replace your reading of *The Old Man and the Sea*. When you're finished reading *The Old Man and the Sea*, and prior to your reading this study guide's critical essays, consider making a bulleted list of what you think are the most important themes and symbols. Write a short paragraph under each bullet explaining why you think that theme or symbol is important; include at least one short quote from the original literary work that supports your contention. Then, test your list and reasons against those found in the following essays. Do you include themes and symbols that the study guide author doesn't? If so, this self test might indicate that you are well on your way to understanding original literary work. But if not, perhaps you will need to re-read *The Old Man and the Sea*.

Hemingway's Style

Hemingway's writing style owes much to his career as a journalist. His use of language—so different from that of, say, his contemporary William Faulkner—is immediately identifiable by most readers. Short words, straightforward sentence structures, vivid descriptions, and factual details combine to create an almost transparent medium for his engaging and realistic stories. Yet without calling attention to itself, the language also resonates with complex emotions and larger and larger meanings—displaying the writer's skill in his use of such subtle techniques as sophisticated patterns; repeated images, allusions, and themes; repeated sounds, rhythms, words, and sentence structures; indirect revelation of historical fact; and blended narrative modes.

In *The Old Man and the Sea*, nearly every word and phrase points to Hemingway's Santiago-like dedication to craft and devotion to precision. Hemingway himself claimed that he wrote on the "principle of the iceberg," meaning that "seven-eighths" of the story lay below the surface parts that show. While the writing in *The Old Man and the Sea* reflects Hemingway's efforts to pare down language and convey as much as possible in as few words as possible, the novella's meanings resonate on a larger and larger scale. The story's brevity, ostensibly simple plot, and distance from much of this period's political affairs all lend the novella a simplistic quality that is as deceptive as it is endearing.

For example, Hemingway conveys one of the novella's central themes by repeatedly yoking religious conviction with a belief in luck. These repeated images and allusions, juxtaposed so often, suggest more than an appropriate sketch of Cuba's Catholic culture, affection for games of chance, and passion for baseball. Both religion and luck rely on ritual and have the power to engender the hope, dreams, faith, absorption, and resolution that ultimately take people beyond themselves. Supporting these repeated images and allusions is the repetition of certain rhythms and sentence structures that signal a kind of ritual or catechism in, for example, the conversations between Santiago and Manolin or the description of Santiago's precise actions in his fishing or in laying out the fish that will nourish him.

Hemingway the journalist also relies on resonances from historical and factual references to enrich the story and advance its themes—a technique used by T. S. Eliot and James Joyce. For example, the novella's many baseball references enabled critics such as C. Harold Hurley and Bickford Sylvester to determine the exact dates in September when the story takes place; to infer a great deal about Cuba's cultural, economic, and social circumstances at the time; and to establish Manolin's exact age. These references do more than provide background information, establish the story's cultural context, and advance the plot. These references also indirectly reveal the characters' motivation, inform the dialogue, and uncover the story's integral thematic dimensions.

Hemingway also relies on blending narrative modes to achieve a shifting psychic distance. The story begins and ends with a third-person, omniscient narration that doesn't dip into Santiago's thoughts. The two parts of the story that take place on land benefit from this controlled reporting. For example, the poignancy of Santiago's circumstances at the story's beginning and the tragedy of his defeat at the story's end are not lost on readers, but instead resonate within them without melodrama because of this psychic distance. On the other hand, the part of the story that takes place at sea draws closer to Santiago's perspective by letting him talk to himself, by presenting a third-person narration of his thoughts, or by drifting subtly from either of these methods into a kind of interior monologue or limited stream of consciousness. This perspective is essential to the story's middle part at sea, which is an odyssey into the natural world, a coming to grips with the natural order, an acceptance of the inevitable cycle of life, and a redemption of the individual's existence. As the transition into Santiago's thoughts seems logical and intuitive because he is alone at sea, with no one to talk to, so does the transition back out again because he returns to land so deeply exhausted.

Themes in the Novella

A commonplace among literary authorities is that a work of truly great literature invites reading on multiple levels or re-reading at various stages in the reader's life. At each of these readings, the enduring work presumably yields extended interpretations and expanded meanings. Certainly, *The Old Man and the Sea* fits that description. The novella invites, even demands, reading on multiple levels.

For example, readers can receive the novella as an engaging and realistic story of Santiago, the old man; Manolin, the young man who loves him; and Santiago's last and greatest battle with a giant marlin. Indeed, Hemingway himself insisted that the story was about a real man and a real fish. Critics have pointed to Hemingway's earlier essay—which mentions a presumably real fisherman who travels far out to sea in a small boat, catches a great fish, and then loses it to sharks—as the seed from which the novella springs.

However, the novella also clearly fits into the category of *allegory*— a story with a surface meaning and one or more under-the-surface meanings; a narrative form so ancient and natural to the human mind as to be universal; a form found in pagan mythology, in both Testaments of the Bible, and in Classical to Post-Modern literature. Likewise, the characters become much more than themselves or even types—they become *archetypes* (universal representations inherited from the collective consciousness of our ancestors and the fundamental facts of human existence).

From this perspective, Santiago is mentor, spiritual father, old man, or old age; and Manolin is pupil, son, boy, or youth. Santiago is the great fisherman and Manolin his apprentice—both dedicated to fishing as a way of life that they were born to and a calling that is spiritually enriching and part of the organic whole of the natural world. Santiago, as the greatest of such fishermen and the embodiment of their philosophy, becomes a solitary human representative to the natural world. He accepts the inevitability of the natural order, in which all creatures are both predator and prey, but recognizes that all creatures also nourish one another. He accepts the natural cycle of human existence as part of that natural order, but finds within himself the imagination and inspiration to endure his greatest struggle and achieve the intangibles that can redeem his individual life so that even when destroyed he can remain undefeated.

In living according to his own code of behavior, accepting the natural order and cycle of life, struggling and enduring and redeeming his individual existence through his life's work, and then passing on to the next generation everything he values, Santiago becomes an *everyman* (an archetypal representation of the human condition). His story becomes everyone's story and, as such, becomes genuinely uplifting. As the tourists who mistake the marlin for a shark still comprehend from its skeleton something of the great fish's grandeur, readers of different ages and levels of understanding can find something inspirational in this story—perhaps even more if they dip into its waters more than once.

Foundations of Behavior

Hemingway's contention that what shows in *The Old Man and the Sea* is just "the tip of the iceberg" seems a particularly accurate assessment of the philosophical and socioeconomic foundations of his characters' behavior. Among the most obvious are the disparate codes that divide the fishermen of Santiago's village into two groups (as critics such as Bickford Sylvester have pointed out).

One group consists of fishermen like Santiago, who respect nature and see themselves as part of it. They rely on their skill and dedication to their craft to participate in nature's eternal pattern. These fishermen are part of a traditional fishing culture that is insulated and isolated from the industrialized world, bereft of modern technology, and bound to extended families and tightly knit communities. These fishermen affectionately refer to the sea as *la mar* (the Spanish feminine) and recognize both its great beauty and its occasional cruelty. As this group's quintessential representative, Santiago performs each fishing task with the precision of a religious ritual and recognizes his kinship with all the living creatures who share a common fate and nourish one another in nature's eternal cycle.

The other group consists of younger, pragmatic fishermen, who exhibit a profound disregard for nature. They do not rely on their own skill, but on mechanisms (such as motorized boats and fishing lines floated by buoys) to ensure a steady income. These fishermen are part of the material progress of a fishing industry, increasingly dependent on the industrialized world for their livelihood, and much less bound to extended families and local communities. These fishermen refer to the sea as *el mar* (the Spanish masculine) and consider it a contestant or an enemy to be overcome. Their philosophy informs behavior that robs the natural world and the dedicated fishermen of intrinsic, less tangible values and spiritually satisfying meaning.

In the philosophical differences between these two groups, Hemingway never implies that Santiago disdains economic security. His poverty, his occasional thoughts about winning the lottery, his musings that the marlin's delicate-tasting flesh would have brought a high price at the market, and so forth all indicate how keenly Santiago feels his own economic circumstances. On the contrary, these philosophical differences help underscore just how keenly Santiago craves the intangibles that give life meaning, provide spiritual enrichment, and ensure the redemption of the individual's existence.

Closely connected to Santiago's recognition of the philosophical differences between the two groups are his Job-like musings. He wonders why sea birds are made so delicate when the ocean can be so cruel, which recalls Job's question about why the innocent are made to suffer (as, of course, Santiago himself is made to suffer). He also wonders why those who let their fishing lines drift are more successful than he is, though he keeps his fishing lines precisely straight, recalling Job's question about why the unworthy prosper. Santiago later answers both questions and more when he considers whether killing the marlin was a great sin. He eventually decides that he killed the marlin not for food, but because he is a fisherman. In his understanding resides the echo of God's answer to Job. Essentially, God's answer was that suffering is in the very nature of the universe. Just as enigmatic, Santiago's own understanding is that he did what he had to do, what he was born to do, and what his role in the eternal nature of things demands. That acceptance is both God's and Santiago's answer to why the good are made to suffer (why the sea birds are made so delicate, why Santiago has gone for so long without a catch) and why the unworthy prosper (why those who let their fishing lines drift are more successful).

As Hemingway makes clear, the pragmatic fishermen (like the scavenger sharks with whom they're associated) inevitably must prevail— at least for a time and in accordance with the natural order that makes all creatures both victors and victims. Yet the philosophy of the pragmatic fishermen also sows the seeds of their own economic destruction. So readers may well infer that Manolin will become much more than just the redeemer of Santiago's understanding of his personal experience at the story's end. Manolin and those who succeed him may well become the standard bearers of a philosophy that eventually must come into its own again, though in a new iteration, after a nearly universal pattern of socioeconomic change (familiar even today among developing nations) has carved itself on the rural Cuban landscape.

CliffsNotes Review

Use this CliffsNotes Review to test your understanding of the original text and reinforce what you've learned in this book. After you work through the review and essay questions, identify the quote section, and the fun and useful practice projects, you're well on your way to understanding a comprehensive and meaningful interpretation of *The Old Man and the Sea*.

Q&A

1. To what is Santiago referring when he tells Manolin, "I know many tricks and I have resolution"? _____

2. Santiago loves the young lion cubs of his dreams as he loves "the boy." To whom is Santiago referring?

   a. Manolin

   b. himself as a young man

   c. both a and b

3. Santiago wonders why birds are made so delicate and fine when the ocean can be so cruel. He also admits that although he keeps his fishing lines straighter than anyone, he has no luck. In both cases, his musings suggest what biblical character? _____

4. What does Santiago call the sea?

   a. *la mar*

   b. *el mar*

   c. *agua grande*

5. Santiago's journey from the land to the sea to the land, the natural order in which all creatures are both predator and prey, and the nature of human existence from youth to old age from generation to generation are all examples of what? _____

Answers: (1) His skill and experience as a fisherman, his dedication to his craft, and his ability to draw self-sustaining inspiration from his own imagination. (2) c. (3) Job. (4) a. (5) Cycles.

Identify the Quote: Find Each Quote in *The Old Man and the Sea*

1. But man is not made for defeat . . . A man can be destroyed but not defeated.

2. *He* didn't beat you. Not the fish.

Answers: (1) [Santiago knows the mutilated marlin will draw other sharks and turn his victory to defeat, yet he also recognizes that, even as all creatures are subject to the natural order that eventually defeats them, human beings have the capacity to redeem their individual existence.] (2) [Manolin explains to Santiago that the marlin did not defeat him, offering Santiago the first indication that his epic struggle and defeat were not a tragedy but a vehicle of individual redemption.]

Essay Questions

1. Consider just some of the literary and biblical characters with whom Santiago is identified. In what ways is he the same and in what ways different?

2. Three times during the novella's conclusion, Manolin expresses his faith in Santiago and all he represents. What do each of these three affirmations represent? Considering that Santiago eventually must die, what role(s) will Manolin assume after Santiago's death and how will Santiago's memory continue to impact Manolin's behavior?

Practice Projects

1. Surf the Internet to see the different online activities devoted to *The Old Man and the Sea*. Once you have an idea of the many ways the developers have chosen to explore this novella, create your own Web site, chat room, bulletin board, photo and/or illustration gallery, Web movie, or other online activity to introduce *The Old Man and the Sea* to other readers. Endeavor to come up with an approach that will attract a new segment of the online audience.

2. Recast a scene from the novella, presenting similar themes and messages but as part of a contemporary story, in a location with which you are familiar, with characters you might meet in your everyday life. Write the scene as if it were part of a new work of fiction or dramatize the scene as if it were part of a new play.

CliffsNotes Resource Center

The learning doesn't need to stop here. CliffsNotes Resource Center shows you the best of the best—links to the best information in print and online about the author and/or related works. And don't think that this is all we've prepared for you; we've put all kinds of pertinent information at www.cliffsnotes.com. Look for all the terrific resources at your favorite bookstore or local library and on the Internet. When you're online, make your first stop www.cliffsnotes.com, where you'll find more incredibly useful information about *The Old Man and the Sea*.

Books

This CliffsNotes book provides a meaningful interpretation of *The Old Man and the Sea*. If you are looking for information about the author and/or related works, check out these other publications:

Hemingway's Debt to Baseball in The Old Man and the Sea: A Collection of Critical Readings, by C. Harold Hurley, brings together essays, excerpts, and elaborations on the role of baseball in Hemingway's greatest novella. Information includes historical facts on the players, managers, games, and events that Hemingway drew upon to establish Manolin's age, set the time period of the work, and advance its action and themes. Lewiston, New York: The Edwin Mellen Press, 1992.

The Old Man and the Sea: Story of a Common Man, by Gerry Brenner, sets the literary and historical context of the novella and provides a close reading of the work that considers structure, character, style, psychology, and biographical matters. Part of the Twayne's Masterworks Studies series. New York: Twayne Publishers, 1991.

Twentieth Century Interpretations of The Old Man and the Sea: A Collection of Critical Essays, edited by Katharine T. Jobes, offers divergent viewpoints and interpretations of the novella. Part of the Twentieth Century Interpretations series. Englewood Cliffs, New Jersey: Prentice Hall, Inc., 1968.

The Cambridge Companion to Hemingway, edited by Scott Donaldson, considers Hemingway's major works, including *The Old Man and the Sea*, in light of gender, fame, journalism, and the political climate of the time. Part of the Cambridge Companions to Literature series. Cambridge: Cambridge University Press, 1996.

Hemingway and the Hispanic World, by Angel Capellán, explores the functions of Spanish history, landscapes, cultural heritage, codes of behavior, politics, rituals, religious mores, and literary traditions in Ernest Hemingway's works, including *The Old Man and the Sea*. Studies in Modern Literature, No. 51. Ann Arbor: UMI Research Press, 1985.

The Politics of Ernest Hemingay, by Stephen Cooper, explores the ambiguities of Hemingway's social and political attitudes and the effects of both on his works, including *The Old Man and the Sea*. Studies in Modern Literature, No. 71. Ann Arbor: UMI Research Press, 1987.

Hemingway: The Final Years, by Michael Reynolds, explores in detail Ernest Hemingway's life and career from 1940 to 1961. New York: W.W. Norton and Company, 1999.

Hemingway: The Critical Heritage, edited by Jeffrey Meyers, offers a representative selection of contemporary criticism on Hemingway's work. Part of The Critical Heritage Series. London: Routledge & Kegan Paul Ltd., 1982.

It's easy to find books published by Wiley Publishing, Inc. You'll find them in your favorite bookstores (on the Internet and at a store near you). We also have three Web sites that you can use to read about all the books we publish:

- www.cliffsnotes.com
- www.dummies.com
- www.wiley.com

Internet

Check out these Web resources for more information about Ernest Hemingway and *The Old Man and the Sea:*

SCORE: The Old Man and the Sea—Teacher Guide, `www.sdcoe.k12.ca.us/score/oldman/oldmantg.html`—This supplemental cyberguide to *The Old Man and the Sea*, created by Barbara Garrison, includes grade-specific student activities. The guide was developed as part of the Schools of California Online Resources for Educators (SCORE) Project, funded by the California Technology Assistance Project (CTAP) and the California County Superintendents Educational Services Association (CCSESA).

SparkNotes: The Old Man and the Sea, `www.sparknotes.com/lit/oldman/`—This site provides context and character information, a summary, analysis, and a section-by-section synopsis with commentary on the novella. Written by Harvard students and graduates, SparkNotes is a member of the iTurf Network.

The Old Man and the Sea Study Questions, `www.metro.net/kjuarez/omts.html`—This site provides a list of study questions on the novella.

Epinions.com: Reviews of The Old Man and the Sea, `www.epinions.com/book_mu-2197653`—This site offers a platform for people who have actually read the book, delivering real opinions, advice, ratings, and reviews. The site provides user biography pages that highlight the people behind the reviews, so viewers know whose opinion to trust.

Next time you're on the Internet, don't forget to drop by `www.cliffsnotes.com`. We created an online Resource Center that you can use today, tomorrow, and beyond.

Films

Check out these films for a broader appreciation of Ernest Hemingway and *The Old Man and the Sea:*

The Old Man and the Sea, Warner Brothers Studios, 1958. This classic feature film, directed by John Sturges, includes a tour-de-force performance by Spencer Tracy as Santiago, the aging fisherman.

The Old Man and the Sea, Pascal Blais Productions, 1999. This short, large-screen format, animated film (animated and directed by Alexander Petrov) won the Academy Award for "Short Film-Animated" on March 27, 2000, in Montreal, Quebec.

Send Us Your Favorite Tips

In your quest for knowledge, have you ever experienced that sublime moment when you figure out a trick that saves time or trouble? Perhaps you realized you were taking ten steps to accomplish something that could have taken two. Or you found a little-known workaround that achieved great results. If you've discovered a useful resource that gave you insight into or helped you understand *The Old Man and the Sea* and you'd like to share it, the CliffsNotes staff would love to hear from you. Go to our Web site at www.cliffsnotes.com and click the Talk to Us button. If we select your tip, we may publish it as part of CliffsNotes Daily, our exciting, free e-mail newsletter. To find out more or to subscribe to a newsletter, go to on the Web.

Index

CliffsNotes

LITERATURE NOTES

CliffsNotes™

The Odyssey
Oedipus Trilogy
Of Human Bondage
Of Mice and Men
The Old Man and
the Sea
Old Testament
Oliver Twist
The Once and
Future King
One Day in the Life of
Ivan Denisovich
One Flew Over
Cuckoo's Nest
100 Years of Solitude
O'Neill's Plays
Othello
Our Town
The Outsiders
The Ox Bow Incident
Paradise Lost
A Passage to India
The Pearl
The Pickwick Papers
The Picture of
Dorian Gray
Pilgrim's Progress
The Plague
Plato's Euthyphro…
Plato's The Republic
Poe's Short Stories
A Portrait of the
Artist…
The Portrait of a Lady
The Power and
the Glory
Pride and Prejudice
The Prince
The Prince and
the Pauper
A Raisin in the Sun
The Red Badge of
Courage
The Red Pony
The Return of the
Native
Richard II
Richard III

The Rise of
Silas Lapham
Robinson Crusoe
Roman Classics
Romeo and Juliet
The Scarlet Letter
A Separate Peace
Shakespeare's
Comedies
Shakespeare's Histories
Shakespeare's
Minor Plays
Shakespeare's Sonnets
Shakespeare's Tragedies
Shaw's Pygmalion &
Arms…
Silas Marner
Sir Gawain…Green
Knight
Sister Carrie
Slaughterhouse-Five
Snow Falling on Cedars
Song of Solomon
Sons and Lovers
The Sound and the Fury
Steppenwolf &
Siddhartha
The Stranger
The Sun Also Rises
T.S. Eliot's Poems &
Plays
A Tale of Two Cities
The Taming of the
Shrew
Tartuffe, Misanthrope…
The Tempest
Tender Is the Night
Tess of the D'Urbervilles
Their Eyes Were
Watching God
Things Fall Apart
The Three Musketeers
To Kill a Mockingbird
Tom Jones
Tom Sawyer
Treasure Island &
Kidnapped
The Trial

Tristram Shandy
Troilus and Cressida
Twelfth Night
Ulysses
Uncle Tom's Cabin
The Unvanquished
Utopia
Vanity Fair
Vonnegut's Works
Waiting for Godot
Walden
Walden Two
War and Peace
Who's Afraid of
Virginia…
Winesburg, Ohio
The Winter's Tale
The Woman Warrior
Worldly Philosophers
Wuthering Heights
A Yellow Raft in
Blue Water

Check Out the All-New CliffsNotes Guides

TECHNOLOGY TOPICS
Balancing Your Check-
book with Quicken
Buying and Selling
on eBay
Buying Your First PC
Creating a Winning
PowerPoint 2000
Presentation
Creating Web Pages
with HTML
Creating Your First
Web Page
Exploring the World
with Yahoo!
Getting on the Internet
Going Online with AOL
Making Windows 98
Work for You

Setting Up a
Windows 98
Home Network
Shopping Online Safely
Upgrading and
Repairing Your PC
Using Your First iMac
Using Your First PC
Writing Your First
Computer Program

PERSONAL FINANCE TOPICS
Budgeting & Saving
Your Money
Getting a Loan
Getting Out of Debt
Investing for the
First Time
Investing in
401(k) Plans
Investing in IRAs
Investing in
Mutual Funds
Investing in the
Stock Market
Managing Your Money
Planning Your
Retirement
Understanding
Health Insurance
Understanding
Life Insurance

CAREER TOPICS
Delivering a Winning
Job Interview
Finding a Job
on the Web
Getting a Job
Writing a Great Resume